Step Stone's

To the Second Greatest Commandment

By Jim Scheeringa

Copyright © 2010 by Jim Scheeringa

Step Stones
To the Second Greatest Commandment
by Jim Scheeringa

Printed in the United States of America

ISBN 9781609577780

All rights reserved solely by the author. The author guarantees all contents are original and do not infringe upon the legal rights of any other person or work. No part of this book may be reproduced in any form without the permission of the author. The views expressed in this book are not necessarily those of the publisher.

Unless otherwise indicated, Bible quotations are taken from The HOLY BIBLE, NEW INTERNATIONAL VERSION®. Copyright © 1973, 1978, 1984 by Biblica. Used by permission of Zondervan; The Holy Bible, New Living Translation. Copyright © 1996, 2004. Used by permission of Tyndale House Publishers, Inc., Wheaton, Illinois 60189; and *The Message.* Copyright © 1993, 1994, 1995, 1996, 2000, 2001, 2002. Used by permission of NavPress Publishing Group.

www.xulonpress.com

To my Mother who had a rough life yet kept her faith, almost as if God used her to prove that His Grace is sufficient. I am sure her prayers for me had a great deal to do with me leaving my prodigal ways. She is now dancing in Heaven with my Father.

To my wonderful and beautiful wife Sandy, her love and patience carried me along many a time. For allowing God's Grace to work through her.

Above all I dedicate this to God who stuck with me by my side even though for a long period I wanted nothing to do with Him. Then He welcomed me back from my prodigal ways with the outstretched arms of

Jesus nailed to the cross. And now when I stumble and fall He is there to gently help me back up.

Contents

Chapter 1   Terrible Times 9
Chapter 2   Black Friday 30
Chapter 3   Christians.......................... 47
Chapter 4   Love Your Neighbor 69
Chapter 5   Stepping Stones 88
Chapter 6   Faith.................................. 98
Chapter 7   Goodness.......................... 116
Chapter 8   Knowledge 131
Chapter 9   Self-Control 144
Chapter 10 Perserverance 161
Chapter 11 Godliness.......................... 186
Chapter 12 Brotherly Kindness 210
Chapter 13 Love a Solid Rock Bridge ... 231
Chapter 14 For This Very Reason 262

Chapter 1

Terrible Times

But mark this: There will be terrible times in the last days. People will be lovers of themselves, lovers of money, boastful, proud, abusive, disobedient to their parents, ungrateful, unholy, without love, unforgiving, slanderous, without self-control, brutal, not lovers of the good, treacherous, rash, conceited, lovers of pleasure rather than lovers of God having a form of godliness but denying its power. 2Timothy 3: 1 – 5a

Terrible times indeed! That's what we are definitely facing. We are currently living through our worst economic recession in a long time. Some say since the great depression. Home foreclosures' are happening at an unheard of rate, unemployment is higher than it's been in the last thirty years, business' are closing up or filing bankruptcy, and financial institutions have become untrustworthy. Our judicial system defends the criminal and tries to discredit the victims. Our government is in a shamble's; their main answer is to spend money they do not have. Not to help matters but the media reports many news items falsely or with hatred.

However, these are national issues; you could say they are larger community issues. Are they the worst our nation has ever seen? I doubt it. Our problems and issues are just getting more and quicker coverage than anytime in history. Are they confined to the United States? Again I doubt it. Do some web searches and I am sure you would find similar issues around the world.

What I believe Paul was warning Timothy about is society and the way the individual thinks and behaves. Warning Timothy and us about what the character of man and the condition of his heart will be during the last days. What I mentioned above, may just be a reflection of man's sinful nature (selfishness) taken to levels never before seen.

Let's look at what Paul warned against.

- *"People will be lovers of themselves"*. This is nothing new, but the level of self love in this society; I would dare to say is unprecedented. I have seen it get much more evident now than thirty years ago, it leaves me shaking my head in disgust. Just look around at the actions of people and hear the words of those around you. The constant message is me, me, me. Go on and do it, you deserve it; if it feels good then it is good. Don't get in their way either, for if you do you will be taken down, pushed out of the way or simply run over. Love of self is listed here first because it leads to all of the other sinful actions mentioned. Love of self is truly the root of all evil.

- *"Lovers of money"*. Again this is nothing new. People have always loved money and it causes so much evil and hurt in our lives and our society. People will do just about anything to get more of it. Look at the crazy reality shows on the television. People will make complete fools of themselves just for a chance to get some money and fame. Look at the amount of money that is spent on lotteries and other gambling, especially by those that can least afford it. I hear all the time "I am ahead on this" or "I am going to do this and that when I hit the jackpot". Then look at the average amount that people are in debt. Not just debt for a home mortgage or a car loan, it goes beyond that. Credit card debt so they can have the best and the newest of everything. The problem with this is that the money that gets spent is money they do not have and so many get so far behind that they end up working far too hard to really enjoy what they have and then losing it all. What ever happened to working for what you get in life? Financial problems are the number one cause of marital and other relationship problems.

- *"Boastful, proud"*. These two just naturally go together. People end up trying to love themselves so much that they believe they can do anything they want. They spend and brag about money they do not have in an effort to keep up with the neighbors. It is all flash to try and impress when it really says that they (think they) are more important than anyone else, even God.

- *"Abusive"*. This word in the Greek should really be translated as blasphemous. When a person is blasphemous, they are taking the name of God in vain. Just watch television for a while, watch a movie, watch the nightly news for that matter and see how often we don't honor God. Evolution! We state as fact that this earth, this universe just happened. Blasphemy. Then there are those that profess to be Christian yet they live and act in ways that you cannot tell them apart from the secular world.

- *"Disobedient to their parents"*. In the last forty years the family has been systematically taken apart. From the school systems taking authority from the parents, to our court system allowing children to divorce their parents. It has happened and will continue to happen. Look at school systems teaching about and passing out birth control without the parents consent or teaching other options. Courts allowing abortions for teen-agers without parental knowledge. Then look at the television sit-coms. They all make the kids smarter and wiser than the parents. Little girls are wiser than the little boys, little boys are wiser than the parents and mom is wiser than dad and dad ends up looking like a babbling idiot no matter what his career may be on the show.

- *"Ungrateful"*. When you look at the disrespect that children have for their parents is it no wonder that we have an ungrateful society. We are always demanding more and more and then we have a government trying to give it to them even though many have not attempted to work for it. Do something for someone that you do not know; something little like open a door for them or let them go first at the checkout line because you have more items than they do. Do you get a spoken thank-you? Hey, I would settle for a smile.
- *"Unholy"*. This means sinful. Look at society in general, look at our government officials, look at television, listen to the songs of all genres, and look at the attitudes of self-love and the love of money. Is it a shock to you that

we are a sinful society and becoming more so as the days go by.

- *"Without love"*. I have seen this translated as heartless and also have seen it translated as without family love. In either case it is very evident in our society. We have all seen stories of homeless people being beaten and even killed just because. We have seen the stories of family members being killed by other family members. I will have more to say about the heartless in chapter two.
- *"Unforgiving"*. I think we can all tell a story or two or more of family members not forgiving another family member for ten, twenty years or more. Many people die with either being not forgiven or not forgiving others. It is a terrible thing to hold a grudge or have a grudge held against you.

- *"Slanderous"*. Look at the media, news being reported from angles of self interest. Words get twisted and words get left out. Look at politicians telling half truths or again twisting words of their opponents so they can look good. Look at your co-workers, your friends. I know I have been cheated and lied about at work. This I can expect but when you get it from friends or family it hurts so much more. All of this falls in the self love category. There seems to be a general attitude of "If it gets me what I want then it is okay to be untruthful".
- *"Without self-control"*. Credit card debt averaging around ten thousand dollars for every person in this country. Buying homes with mortgage payments more than they earn. This is a lack of self control on the individual

because they want to appear to have everything and on the mortgage company because they need to have more. I personally have known individuals with more than one hundred twenty thousand dollars in credit card debt not counting car payments, mortgages, school loans, etc. Then of course there is the drug addiction, alcoholism, food addictions that are other signs of no self-control. These usually follow the out of control action of spending what you do not have.

- *"Brutal"*. Criminal brutality has never been worse. Every day you hear on the news some horrendous crime and the law enforcement officials say that is the worst they have ever seen. Children being beaten and sexually abused by adults and other children. I recently heard of a mother that beheaded and cannibalized her own three and a half week old baby. Yes that is right three and a half weeks old. She said the devil told her to do it. Pure evil! Makes my heart cry out in agony. It does every time I hear stories like this. Then there is a surge in almost full term pregnant women being killed and their unborn baby being taken from them usually by another woman that wants a baby in order to keep a man. Senseless!

- *"Not lovers of the good, treacherous, rash, conceited, lovers of pleasure rather than lovers of God"*. God gets left out of all our walks of life. When you think of this, think gossip, jumping to conclusions, not trusting anyone or anything, thinking higher of yourself than one should. So much anger is in our society. Anger at how you were raised. Anger at God for not giving you a better life. Perpetrators become the victims and victims do not get justice. Those that speak up against such things are labeled as hypocrites, mean spirited or just plain stupid. Name calling in our public life has become a way of life. There is no respect yet all cry out for the respect. Trouble is we want the respect before we will give it. What ever happened to earning our respect? We have taken God out of our nation, our community, our schools and our lives. All we have to do is take a look to the Old Testament and see the history of the Israelites to see what happens when you take God out of the equation. With self love, love of money more than anything else, pride, disobedience, ungratefulness, unforgiving and unholy attitudes, not having love, slandering, lack of self control, brutality, what do you expect? It seems to me that goodness is looked down upon by all, at least by the vocal people. Our society ends up celebrating deceit and arrogance. There is no loyalty anymore, no common sense and loving pleasure or what seems pleasurable is the end product of all of this.

- *"Having a form of godliness but denying its power"*. In all of our society's problems, with all of our nation's problems we have a group of people known as the elites that try to tell us how to live. They believe they have moral authority because they have much or have positions of power and that makes them "knowledgeable" and the trouble is, many regular folks listen to what they say and believe it. Oh sure! What they say sounds good and it may even be good; but then they turn around and deny God. They will say things such as "There is no right or wrong, you just try to do your best." Does this make sense to you? It doesn't to me. Then we have "Christian's" that do horrible things such as take advantage of the elderly, abusing children, extorting large companies or wealthy individuals. These wolves in sheep's clothing get a lot of negative attention. Then people end up painting all Christians with that same brush. "Denying its power" really is the feeling that no one, not even God has the right to tell us what to do.

With these characteristics listed by Paul are a series of what appears to be opposites. For example with self love comes self hatred driven by the self love. With the love of money comes depression from either over spending or what seems to be a feeling of never having enough. With the disobedience of parents (authority) comes a complete lack of guidance and a feeling of being overwhelmed or even lost. With ungratefulness comes the inability to see good even in your loved ones. This then leads to the inability to love others because you think they do not love you. You become unforgiving because you believe others don't forgive your errors so you don't need to forgive them; (most of the time though it is failure to see your errors in the first place). Then what naturally follows if left unchecked is the lack of self-control, slandering, brutality, conceitedness, etc. How else would you explain the abundance of little girls and now little boys with anorexia, bulimia, young people in their adolescence with drug addictions, alcohol abuse, sexual addictions, depression, and these all carry on into the adult years. Sometimes these are hidden emotional problems which can haunt a person and their loved ones, destroying themselves and those that care about them. I know, I came from these attitudes.

1 Peter 5: 8b states this; *"Your enemy the devil prowls around like a roaring lion looking for someone to devour."* The devil has been able through his lying schemes to turn mankind into a messed up bunch. You see he is a smooth talking liar and we tend to believe those types. So when you take a God given personality trait such as love of self, the devil has pounced and turned it into a path of destruction. That path is the love of money, pride, blasphemy, on and on down Paul's warning list. Whoever falls onto that path (I have) will be devoured. What saved

me of course was Jesus through the prayers of my mother and others.

Paul then goes on and tells Timothy and me in verse 5b of chapter 3 in his second letter. *"Have nothing to do with them."* Then further warns in verses 6 - 9 *"They are the kind who worm their way into homes... who are loaded down with sins and are swayed by all kinds of evil desires, always learning but never able to acknowledge the truth...these men oppose the truth—men of depraved minds, who, as far as the faith is concerned, are rejected. But they will not get very far because...their folly will be clear to everyone."* Paul is saying that the traits listed above are traits of evil secular men and women. We are not to have anything to do with them, we might be devoured.

Is this a contradiction to what Jesus commanded the disciples to do?

"Then Jesus came to them and said, "All authority in heaven and on earth has been given to me. Therefore go and make disciples of all nations, baptizing them in the name of the Father and of the Son and of the Holy Spirit, and teaching them to obey everything I have commanded you. And surely I am with you always, to the very end of the age.""
Matthew 28: 18 – 20?

I don't think it is a contradiction. I believe that Paul is telling Timothy to be watchful and very careful not to hang around with these types. It was also a warning that if these type of men and women get into the church they can corrupt the whole body. Paul wrote this in 1 Corinthians 15: 33 *"Do not be misled: Bad company corrupts good character."* Paul knew that Timothy would have to be in the world to carry out the great commission and the best way for him to make an impression would be to live his life as Jesus lived, and not get caught up in the ways of the world. Jesus also knew this because in his commission at the very end he said *"surely I am with you always, to the very end of the age."* What a great comfort.

So what am I to do then? Live my life and pray, allowing myself to be led by the Holy Spirit. Pray that Jesus would empower me to be myself, to be strong, and remember that I am his representative and the world is watching. Always knowing that through the Holy Spirit, Jesus is with me giving me the strength. So I say pray and then pray some more. Pray for family and friends, my communities, my church, my Christian brothers and sisters around the world, this society, for this nation, for our leaders, our world. Pray with the knowledge that what I am going through may just be God's will, (why else would it be in the Bible?), I do not know; but continue to pray seeking the truth of God's will.

Is this the end of the world? I do not know and will never profess to know. Many people have made predictions and all of them have been wrong. Many predictions are still being made and they too will be wrong. No man knows the time when the end will be. Just read Matthew chapters 24 and 25 about this. The end will be like the days of Noah, life will be happening as normal. The end will come like a thief in the night so be prepared. If someone claims to know the end date, get away from them before they corrupt you also.

Other readings for study:
Luke 21, Romans 1: 18 – 32,

Chapter 2

Black Friday

Black Friday is now commonly known as the Friday after Thanksgiving. We know it as the opening day of the Christmas shopping season. The term originated in Philadelphia, PA, ironically known as the "City of Brotherly Love". The police, cab-drivers, and bus drivers started calling that day "Black Friday" in 1966 because of the terrible traffic congestion and the generally poor attitudes of people.

Here is a story for you from something that happened on "Black Friday" in Valley

Stream, Long Island, NY on November 28, 2008. (Names are left out.) A story that makes me sad and angry, but it does demonstrate what Paul told us in his letter to Timothy about the end times being terrible.

A Wal-Mart worker died early Friday after an "out-of-control" mob of frenzied shoppers smashed through the Long Island store's front doors and trampled him. The Black Friday stampede plunged the Valley Stream outlet into chaos, knocking several employees to the ground and sending others scurrying atop vending machines to avoid the horde. When the madness ended, a 34-year-old employee was dead and four shoppers, including a woman eight months pregnant, were injured. "He was bum-rushed by 200 people," said a Wal-Mart worker. "They took the doors off the hinges. He was trampled and killed in front of me. They took me down; too ... I didn't know if I was going to live through it. I literally had to fight people off my back," the employee said.

The employee a temporary maintenance worker was gasping for air as shoppers continued to surge into the store after its 5 a.m. opening, witnesses said. Even officers who arrived to perform CPR on the trampled worker were stepped on by wild-eyed shoppers streaming inside, a cop at the scene said. "They pushed him down and walked all over him," his sobbing sister, said. "How could these people do that? He was such a young man with a good heart, full of life. He didn't deserve that." His sister said doctors told the family he died of a heart attack. His cousin, called the circumstances "completely unacceptable", and said "his body was a stepping bag with so much disregard for human life. There has to be some accountability."

Roughly 2,000 people gathered outside the Wal-Mart's doors in the predawn darkness. Chanting "push the doors in," the crowd pressed against the glass as the clock ticked down to the 5 a.m. opening. Sensing catastrophe, nervous employees formed a human chain inside the entrance to slow down the mass of shoppers. It didn't work. The mob barreled in and overwhelmed workers. "They were jumping over the barricades and breaking down the door," said one of the customers "Everyone was screaming. You just had to keep walking on your toes to keep from falling over."

After the throng toppled the employee his fellow employees had to fight through the crowd to help him, police said. A witness said shoppers acted like "savages and when they were saying they had to leave, that an employee got killed, people were yelling, 'I've been in line since Friday morning! They kept shopping."

When paramedics arrived, the employee's condition was grave. "They were pumping his chest, trying to bring him back, and there was nothing," said a Wal-Mart worker. The employee was taken to Franklin Hospital and pronounced dead at 6:03 a.m.

The president of Wal-Mart's northeast division said the company took extraordinary safety precautions. "We expected a large crowd this morning and added additional internal security, additional third-party security, additional store associates and we worked closely with the Nassau County police," he said in a statement. "We also erected barricades. Despite all of our precautions, this unfortunate event occurred."

The 28-year-old pregnant woman and three other shoppers were taken to area hospitals with minor injuries, police said.

In a news conference after the incident, Nassau County police spokesman described the crowd as "out of control" and the scene as "utter chaos." He said Wal-Mart did not have enough security on hand and said criminal charges were possible but that it would be difficult to identify individual shoppers in surveillance videos.

Items on sale at the Wal-Mart store included a $798 Samsung 50-inch Plasma HDTV, a Bissell Compact Upright Vacuum for $28 and Men's Wrangler Tough Jeans for $8.

The Long Island store reopened at 1 p.m. and was packed within minutes.

"I look at these people's faces and I keep thinking one of them could have stepped on him," said one employee. "How could you take a man's life to save $20 on a TV?"

(FoxNews.com)

How low we have sunk. Let's look at what happened comparing it with what Paul warned about.

- Love of self – They yelled saying that they were in line for a long time and they now deserve to be shopping even though a man was dead and four others injured.
- Love of money – All of this incivility for a savings of a few dollars. Sure the country was coming off sky high gas prices that hurt everyone and they were looking to save a few dollars; but at what price? To possibly have a man's life on your hands?
- Boastful, Pride – I am sure these traits had a lot to do with it. I can hear the bragging now; "Wal-Mart only had a few of those televisions and I got one".

- Abusive – Remember this should really be translated as blasphemous. How could you be more blasphemous than to disregard a human life that was created by God for a few dollars saved?
- Disobedient to their parents – In this case it was disobedience to authority. Even though there was crowd control it was of no use. Trampling on the paramedics, continuing to shop even though they were asked to leave. It all started with their parents and their selfishness.
- Ungrateful – They had an opportunity to save some money. What did they do? They were ungrateful for this and pushed the doors in before the store opened. "Chanting push the doors in" as they pressed against them.

- Unholy – Most definitely a sinful act no matter whose rules you live by. Enough said!
- Without love – The only love they exhibited was love of self and money.
- Unforgiving – Total disregard to the store employees and other authorities by not leaving the store when asked because an employee was killed and they continued to shop. A definite act of an unforgiving attitude. Unforgiving of those that requested they come back later and that this would inconvenience them.
- Slanderous – I do not know for sure; but I would bet there was a lot of denial when asked if they saw anything or knew who did this.
- With out self-control – Yes! Again enough said.

- Brutal – How much more brutal can you get? Jumping over barricades and breaking the doors down then trampling an employee, four shoppers including an eight month pregnant women, walking over the rescue workers, and getting angry when asked to leave. No description fits except brutality.
- Not lovers of the good – No goodness was found in this crowd.
- Treacherous – These people do not realize it; but they were treacherous to themselves (conscious) and to a civilized society.
- Conceited, lovers of pleasure rather than lovers of God – Driven by their conceit (self love) God was nowhere to be found in this crowd.
- Having a form of godliness but denying its power – I would guess that many

> if not all of the people involved in this group think of themselves as a good person. Show me the godliness in this. It only came after it was all over.
> - Have nothing to do with them – You bet I wont.

This was just one incident. You can look around on the web and see stories of a lesser magnitude, yet just as horrific that can fall into this category. Stories of people getting run over and no one stopping to help and witnesses just standing there not even lifting their cell phone to call for help. I am sure I could do a few web searches and find enough examples to fill this book. It does remind me of a story that many have heard before. It is called "The Good Samaritan". It is a parable that Jesus taught and it is found in Luke 10: 30 – 35

In reply Jesus said: "A man was going down from Jerusalem to Jericho, when he fell into the hands of robbers. They stripped him of his clothes, beat him and went away, leaving him half dead. A priest happened to be going down the same road, and when he saw the man, he passed by on the other side. So too, a Levite, when he came to the place and saw him, passed by on the other side. But a Samaritan, as he traveled, came where the man was; and when he saw him, he took pity on him. He went to him and bandaged his wounds, pouring on oil and wine. Then he put the man on his own donkey, took him to an inn and took care of him. The next day he took out two silver coins and gave them to the innkeeper. 'Look after him,' he said, 'and when I return, I will reimburse you for any extra expense you may have.'

Who were the people in the Wal-Mart store? Were they the Samaritan? Certainly not! They fell into the category of the Priest and the Levite. When these two passed the beaten man they probably made excuses to not help him. Maybe the excuses sounded like this: "I am by myself, what can I do?" "I am in a hurry." "Maybe somebody else will help him." "I might get hurt also."

I would guess there were people at the Wal-Mart store saying the same kind of things. "Somebody else will help him." "What can I do?" "I don't know first aid." "I will get injured also." "I got to get that television, there are only a few of them here." There could be many more but you get the picture.

I wonder about what the Priest and Levite thought about later on, if anything at all. I also wonder about these shoppers at the Wal-Mart store. How many went home and prayed a prayer of remorse? How many went home and was appalled at their actions? How many went home with no remorse at all? How many went home not knowing anything happened at all until they heard it on the news? Then what did they think? We will never know for sure.

Then I wonder about Christianity. Were any of these people that stormed through the door killing one man and injuring four others proclaiming to be Christians? Statistically they were. According to recent polls on the status of religion in this country seventy-six percent of the people identified with Christianity. This figure was down a little since 2001 but it is still a substantial number.

In the Wal-Mart incident there were an estimated two hundred shoppers that stampeded the door. If you take just sixty percent proclaiming to be Christian then that would mean that one hundred and twenty of those shoppers were "Christian", and did not stop to help. They looked after their own self interest.

I am not meaning to be judge here; I am just trying to get a handle on this horrible incident. It pains me even more to think that many potential "Christians" were part of that.

Our President recently proclaimed to the Arab world that the United States is not a Christian nation. I disagreed with him when he said that, and I am not sure he actually meant that. He may have been trying to gain political momentum. I don't know for sure. Again it is not my place to judge.

Then I look at this "Black Friday" incident, I wonder if maybe our President was correct. Maybe we are no longer a "Christian" nation. Maybe we just like to think we are because we do not want to share our true selves with anyone or we are ashamed at our true self. It is not our government that makes us "Christian" but our society, our communities, each of as individuals that would make us what we were founded to be. Maybe instead we have become a nation of "Pharisees". "Pharisees" that have lost our touch with God and what it means to be a child of God.

When Jesus walked this earth, he had many confrontations with the religious leaders of his day. Just look how he thought about them in his story of "The Good Samaritan". Remember his words when he called the religious leaders "whitewashed tombs". Jesus was referring to their attitudes of being all high and mighty on the outside but inside they were dead. Dead to God's true calling, dead to compassion, dead to mercy and grace. This was the complete opposite of God. God throughout history had been extremely compassionate and longsuffering (patient) with the Israelites.

This only wants me to take a look at what a "Christian" truly is. Maybe just maybe we are missing something. Maybe just maybe we aren't being taught what we need to know as "Christians". Then again, maybe we have fallen into self absorption and self love deeper than any one imagined and that we truly are in the terrible times that Paul warned Timothy and us about.

Other readings for study:

Matthew 12: 22 – 37, Matthew 15: 1 – 28, Psalm 12

Chapter 3

Christians

The disciples were called Christians first at Antioch. Acts 11: 26b

Let me be clear here before I go any further. I am not trying to be a judge or even sound judgmental. I even feared writing this because some people might remember things of my past and claim I have no place in writing this. That was my past. I live for the present and the future that I hope and pray will be to the glory of God. Much of what I am writing I am writing for myself, to teach myself and prayerfully I hope will open the eyes of others. You see much of what I plan on writing (if God takes me that direction), I have personally experienced. I was raised in a Christian family but did not see much Christianity in my church, Christian school, or Christian community. I became very aware of the wrong attitudes and I guess I grew a set of "Pharisee" antennae. I was keenly aware of those who were putting on shows to appear "Christian". I ended up calling them "Churchians" in my own mind (with a smug). In other words I did not regard "Christians" very well. You know the ones that I am talking about. They are extremely judgmental and at the same time will overlook actions and attitudes of people that seem important to them or their church. They feel they are better than everyone else. In essence they have an attitude of not sharing the grace that was so abundantly shared with them. If you looked different, smelled different, talked different, you were treated as not having the opportunity to share that same grace. You were beneath them. I saw them as "Pharisee's".

Let me define a Pharisee from a few thoughts from Jesus about them and how they acted:

- Loved to pray out loud with long prayers and with many words.
- Loved to dress up in the finest clothes (whitewashed tombs).
- Loved to pray out on the street corners to try and show how holy they were.
- Loved to condemn others for not being like them yet not doing anything to help those less fortunate than them.
- Loved to make themselves first, sit at the head of the banquet tables.

- Loved to be called Rabbi, given a title of honor.
- Loved to worship the temple and the laws instead of God who was the reason for the temple in the first place.
- Loved to follow the law to the entirety, condemning those that do not, yet at the same time neglecting mercy, grace, and patience that God has showed the Israelites throughout their entire history.
- Loved to dig out the speck in their brother's eye while walking around with a two-by-four in their own eye.
- Loved to try and trap Jesus by their own double speak.
- Loved to criticize Jesus because he hung out with sinners.

I saw many of these same characteristics in the church and it disgusted me. None of what I saw and experienced in the church was what I read about in the Bible. This drove me away from the church and I had the attitude that much of the world has today about "Christianity". An attitude that asked where is the love that "Christians" proclaim to have? Where is the love of Jesus that he taught about?

I thought to myself that if this is what being a "Christian" is all about, I want nothing to do with it. I will continue to believe in God, yet live my life as the world does. After all I was finding more acceptance in the world than I did in church. I use the word acceptance now, but back then I thought it was love, it was not. I went about my merry way causing havoc in my life and those around me, continuing this pattern for twenty plus years.

Then during a stormy period in my life, God through his grace allowed me to find Him, and He encouraged me to try church once again. I argued with God a lot about this, but eventually (several years) I broke down and went. I tried a small church that was not of the same denomination I grew up in. In this little independent church, I found something different; I found acceptance just the way I was. I expected (based on my previous experience) that this church and its members would expect me to change and be like them before I was accepted. How much more wrong could I have been. You see God wants you now, not after you change, He will provide the change mechanism which is the Holy Spirit. For if it was left up to us, we would not change and we would just waste away with no hope of peace.

I started going to church regularly, but life in the world taught me to be aware of those with false pretenses. So I polished up my set of "Pharisee" antennae and put them on. Oh yea I did spot the "Pharisee's" pretty easily I must say and was actually proud of it. I was saddened and disheartened to learn that there was so many "Pharisee's" around. We moved to a different part of the country and my antennae were in overtime. The church my wife and I decided on was a little larger but also had more "Pharisees" in it than the church before, and some of them were far more obvious (no details). So after a couple of years we switched to a different church; a church that was of a completely different style than what we were used to.

One day God, through another personal trial, (which happened shortly before we switched churches) reveled to me that by keeping up my "Pharisee" antennae, I was actually being a "Pharisee" myself. That I was judging those that did not meet my expectations of what a "Christian" should be or what I thought they should do. God showed me that I was using the word churchian in a derogatory way and in doing so I was guilty of lumping all into one judgmental category. In other words I was keeping my eyes on what others were doing and not on Jesus.

This brings me back to the opening verse. When I first read this verse I thought it was a good term one that means simply belonging to Christ Jesus. It does mean that; but the commentaries I have since read reveal that the people of Antioch were using it in a derogatory manner, in an insulting way much the same way I once regarded Christians. You see the disciples and those that believed were living a different life style than the other citizens of Antioch. In the earlier verses of Acts 11, it tells us that some disciples started teaching Greeks in Antioch about Jesus and many believed. When the disciples in Jerusalem heard about this they went to Antioch to see what was going on. They found the evidence that the grace of God was at work and so they stayed and taught many more about Jesus and many more believed and turned to the Lord. Thus they became different from what they were before. They changed how they lived their life. The sinful lifestyle that they used to live, they now forsook. So their friends and even family ridiculed them and shunned them. Just like today those with hardened hearts (as mine was), will look at anything different from themselves as wrong. So being called a "Christian" in Antioch was meant to be an insult but instead it turned out to be a badge of honor. Our society does that again and sadly many of us allow it.

The disciples did not pick and chose the right people to teach. They taught whoever would listen. They taught about Jesus, recalling what Jesus taught them. It did not matter what social level, what education level, how much money they made, or what kinds of clothes they wore. All were welcome, all were loved; and that I feel may be the single thing wrong with many individual churches today. Not all people are treated with love and love was the main topic that Jesus taught about. When Jesus went around healing hundreds of people maybe thousands, it was all about love and glorifying the name of his and our heavenly Father.

To demonstrate how different the Christians in Antioch were, here is a scripture passage of the first Christians in Jerusalem.

All the believers were one in heart and mind. No one claimed that any of his possessions was his own, but they shared everything they had. With great power the apostles continued to testify to the resurrection of the Lord

Jesus, and much grace was upon them all. There were no needy persons among them. For from time to time those who owned lands or houses sold them, brought the money from the sales and put it at the apostles' feet, and it was distributed to anyone as he had need. Acts 4: 33 - 35

After all why would the disciples teach the Christians in Antioch any different than they did in Jerusalem? Why would they act differently in Antioch then they did in Jerusalem? Many of them probably had to choose between their new faith full of grace and love and their family and old way of life. It was about love, helping each other out. The same happens still today. Now I am not suggesting that all Christians sell their possessions, or live together in isolated communities because that is not the reason the first Christians acted in this manner. They acted in this way because they were being put out of the synagogues and temples.

They were in essence being discriminated against because they were following Jesus and so many could not get jobs to support themselves and their families. It was for this reason they pulled their resources together so they could survive. It was love for Jesus and each other. I am not sure that if the same was happening today that we would do the same. Not in this country at least. We are probably seeing it out in the mission fields in the poorer nations were there is teaching about Jesus and the promise of salvation that comes with belief and repentance.

Let's look at the teaching of Jesus: Just prior to him telling the parable of "The Good Samaritan" we find this:

On one occasion an expert in the law stood up to test Jesus. "Teacher," he asked, "what must I do to inherit eternal life?" "What is written in the Law?" he replied. "How do you read it?" He answered: " 'Love the Lord your God with all your heart and with all your soul and with all your strength and with all your mind'; and, 'Love your neighbor as yourself.'" "You have answered correctly," Jesus replied. *"Do this and you will live."* Luke 10: 25 – 28

The second greatest commandment was to love your neighbor as yourself. To demonstrate how important that message was in the life of Jesus and then his disciples, here is a sampling of scripture passages that show just that along with a little highlight of that scripture:

- Matthew 5: 43 – 47 loving your enemies as well as your brother.
- Matthew 22: 39 & Mark 12: 31 second greatest commandment, loving your neighbor as yourself.
- Luke 10: 27 this is the parable of "The Good Samaritan"
- John 15: 9 – 17 remaining in Jesus love and love each other.

- Romans 12: 9 – 10 love must be sincere and being devoted to one another in brotherly love.
- Romans 13: 8 – 10 love is the fulfillment of the law.
- 1 Corinthians 13 is the clear definition of what love is and if you do not have love then you are a nothing. It also states that three characteristics remain: faith hope and love, with love being the greatest.
- Galatians 5: 14 the entire law is summed up in love your neighbor as yourself.
- Ephesians 4: 2 bearing with one another in love.
- Ephesians 5: 2 live a life imitating Jesus, living a life of love.
- Hebrews 13: 1 -2 love each other and entertain strangers for they may actually be angels.

- 1 John 3: 18 love not with words, but by actions and in truth.

In the beginning of this chapter I told of my early life experience in church and felt that "Christians" were far too judgmental. Here is a passage from James that demonstrates just what I felt and I fear still happens far too often today.

My brothers, as believers in our glorious Lord Jesus Christ, don't show favoritism. Suppose a man comes into your meeting wearing a gold ring and fine clothes, and a poor man in shabby clothes also comes in. If you show special attention to the man wearing fine clothes and say, "Here's a good seat for you," but say to the poor man, "You stand there" or "Sit on the floor by my feet," have you not discriminated among yourselves and become judges with evil thoughts? Listen, my dear brothers: Has not God chosen those who are poor in the eyes of the world to be rich in faith and to inherit the kingdom he promised those who love him? But you have insulted the poor. Is it not the rich who are exploiting you? Are they not the ones who are dragging you into court? Are they not the ones who are slandering the noble name of him to whom you belong? If you really keep the royal law found in Scripture, "Love your neighbor as yourself," you are doing right. But if you show favoritism, you sin and are convicted by the law as lawbreakers. For whoever keeps the whole law and yet stumbles at just one point is guilty of breaking all of it. James 2: 1 - 10

Notice "Love your neighbor as yourself" is called the royal law. I not only have seen this behavior listed in James but have also had this happen to me. Many churches still today want their membership to dress in a certain manner. Let me say there is nothing wrong with dressing up nicely, but what is the attitude that you express to others around you that may not have the nice clothes or feel that their freedom in Christ allows them to be the person that God created them to be. Other churches feel you have to worship the way they do or you have it wrong.

The church I grew up in was part of a large denomination that mainly reached out to people of a particular national heritage. As a child, I witnessed people of Asian descent enter our church and the whispering was deafening. How do you think that made those people feel? I witnessed some women tell my mother (a recent widow trying to raise a family) that she needs to dress better. I was shunned as I got older because of the length of my hair (among a few other things) and witnessed this among many others also. Instead of reaching out to me to try and use my personality and those of the others for Christ, we were rejected. It's as if you could not have a hope of salvation unless you followed these man made regulations. It comes down to legalism in the churches, the same as the "Pharisee's". (If a church puts a lot of emphasis on thou shalt's, then there may be a problem and should be addressed in prayer with God.)

Does anyone out there that behaves in this manner really believe that Jesus who taught against the social discrimination of the Pharisees only reached out to those that had money and dressed properly? I doubt it; yet many members of churches and even some churches as an organization are doing exactly that without giving it much thought.

Jesus in Matthew 23 listed "seven woes" as he talked about and preached against the Pharisees and their attitudes. (Some of what I listed earlier in the definition of Pharisee is found here.) Here is just one example of what Jesus said about the Pharisee's that describes what I have been writing about.

"In the same way, on the outside you appear to people as righteous but on the inside

you are full of hypocrisy and wickedness. Matthew 23: 28

Modern example: In Kansas (I believe) there is a church that I would describe as a cult. They go around declaring that the young brave soldiers that died in either the Iraq or Afghanistan wars are going to hell because they fought for a country that they say is at war with God. They can stand there and act all righteous, yet at the same time are full of hypocrisy. You see they refuse to share the grace that was so abundantly shared with the entire world (not a select few) by the cross of Jesus.

Let me be clear. I believe that there are far more good, honest Christians in today's churches than there are "Pharisees". I think that the "Pharisees" are noticed more often than the others working many times quietly in the background. Then again some honest Christians may just be afraid to speak up because of the ridicule they will face if they speak against the "Pharisees". Or they may fear the "knowledge" of these "leaders". You see many of these people will know the Bible inside and out better than most. Many will twist scripture to meet their own beliefs and desires. I also believe that if the churches started sharing the grace and overlooking our own personal opinions (after all we are just weak flesh), then we can make a difference. But as long as there are "ministries" such as that in Kansas, there will be many that will refuse to take Christianity serious.

Earlier I mentioned that recent polls show that seventy percent of the American population identifies themselves as Christian; however only forty percent say they attend church. The pollsters have actually found that in truth only about twenty percent actually do attend church. They found that many people answer polls in ways they think is the proper answer, not the truth. So where does the problem lie? Is it in the church? Is it in people's hearts and attitudes? I believe there is something missing. What is it you ask? The answer can be found in the "Second Greatest Commandment", love your neighbor as yourself.

Again please let me be clear about this. I am not trying to judge or condemn. My only desire is to see the name of Jesus lifted high, and that God the Father will be glorified. I am also not trying to sound like I have it all together and have found perfection in my life, for I have not. Yet it is something I strive for. I have found (and still find) that a lot of those old things I was and things that I did creeping in on me trying to make me stumble, sometimes I do. Now that I am a Christian the most awesome thing is that when I stumble, God lovingly through his grace leans down and helps me back up as long as I reach my hand out to Him. Then He encourages me to continue along with him in the peace and joy of his grace.

Other readings for study:

Matthew 23, the other passages listed above concerning the "Second Greatest Commandment". Psalms 73

Chapter 4

Love Your Neighbor

He answered: " 'Love the Lord your God with all your heart and with all your soul and with all your strength and with all your mind'; and, 'Love your neighbor as yourself.'" "You have answered correctly," Jesus replied. "Do this and you will live." But he wanted to justify himself, so he asked Jesus, "And who is my neighbor?" Luke 10: 27 - 29

Just a thought here, maybe just maybe we have become so absorbed with trying to love ourselves that we have lost the ability to really understand what love is, and have instead ended up hating ourselves. So we talk bad to our self and end up treating others with contempt and disrespect in an effort to lift our self higher. After all most of us would not talk to or treat our neighbors the way we talk to or treat ourselves. We end up being nice to our neighbors yet at the same time despising them. Maybe because we think we are better than them or we think they think they are better than us.)

Just who is my neighbor? Wow! That is a loaded question. I am sure it means those living near me, does it not? I then have to ask the following:

- What about the old cranky guy or woman across the street that is always yelling about the neighborhood kids or pets?
- What about the people next door that do not keep up their yard very nice and they just seem kind of weird?

- What about the young couple down the street that has cars coming in and out at all hours of the day? Playing their music so loud squealing their tires. I hear they are not even married, they just live together!
- What about the woman always yelling and beating her kids? She is home alone all the time because her husband is in jail for drugs. She and her kids don't have much of anything but they are always so dirty and when you try talking to her she seems short with her answers and acts like you are intruding on her. Could it be she is frightened, embarrassed, ashamed, or all of these?
- What about the man at the end of the block whose wife left him for another woman? There just had to be something weird going on there. Maybe he

did something that drove her away. What about those kids growing up in that environment? What will they turn out to be? The oldest girl I think she is eleven tries to take care of the other two but she can only do so much.

(You found out about all of the above by talking to the "good" neighbors.)

- What about that crabby clerk at the gas station? Never a good thing to say about anything. Just complaining all the time.
- What about the driver on the cell phone that was not paying attention that just pulled out in front of me? He didn't even know I was there?
- What about the people driving in the middle lane ten miles under the speed limit blocking all the other traffic as they go?

- What about my boss that can never appreciate what I do?
- What about my co-worker that wants to screw around all day long?
- What about my employee that comes in late all the time?
- What about the drunk on the park bench or the crack prostitute on the corner? Man they are just dirty and smelly.

I could go on and on but I think you get the message. It all leads to what I believe is some fundamental teachings of Jesus that largely goes ignored or given some glance over attempts at best. That is the love that Christians are supposed to share unconditionally.

I have referenced the parable of "The Good Samaritan" several times now but this is worth repeating:

In reply Jesus said: "A man was going down from Jerusalem to Jericho, when he fell into the hands of robbers. They stripped him of his clothes, beat him and went away, leaving him half dead. A priest happened to be going down the same road, and when he saw the man, he passed by on the other side. So too, a Levite, when he came to the place and saw him, passed by on the other side. But a Samaritan, as he traveled, came where the man was; and when he saw him, he took pity on him. He went to him and bandaged his wounds, pouring on oil and wine. Then he put the man on his own donkey, took him to an inn and took care of him. The next day he took out two silver coins and gave them to the innkeeper. 'Look after him,' he said, 'and when I return, I will reimburse you for any extra expense you may have.' "Which of these three do you think was a neighbor to the man who fell into the hands of robbers?" The expert in the law replied, "The one who had mercy on him." Jesus told him, "Go and do likewise." Luke 10: 30 – 37

I feel that much of the preaching today amounts to cheerleading for God, not all but some very prominent preaching. Please don't misunderstand me, this is all good, but it seems that most sermons are telling us how much God loves us. The sermons are geared towards telling us that God is not bad. That God wants the very best for us. That God wants us to prosper (make us rich). That God wants us to be happy. All of this is true by the way, and I praise God for these. What I am trying to say is there is so much more that God wants from us. Look at what I just listed as sermon topics. They are all about us which leads right back to the first warning Paul gave Timothy about the terrible times. "People will be lovers of themselves." People want to hear about the good things that God will give them if we follow Him. Again this is true because if our hearts are in the right place God will bless us beyond our imagination. I say it again please don't misunderstand me all of this is good but there is more and we need to be teaching that.

Look at the list at the beginning of this chapter about who is my neighbor. We still as a church (God's people) end up with way too many judgmental thoughts. Look at what Paul writes to us in Romans:

You, therefore, have no excuse, you who pass judgment on someone else, for at whatever point you judge the other, you are condemning yourself, because you who pass judgment do the same things. Now we know that God's judgment against those who do such things is based on truth. So when you, a mere man, pass judgment on them and yet do the same things, do you think you will escape God's judgment? Romans 2: 1 – 3

Paul is writing this to the relatively new believers (Christians) in Rome. He was trying to teach them some of the basic fundamentals of following Jesus and his teachings. We should not judge another for gossiping, for being smelly, for not dressing right, for going to a different denomination, or for worshipping in a way you are unfamiliar with. When we make a judgment on someone without knowing them or their story, we make ourselves really look silly. Remember the world is watching. Before I go on I must confess these are some of my stumbling points and my flesh falls into behaving in this manner and I pray for forgiveness when I feel the Holy Spirit convict me.

There is more. Again Paul writes us in Romans:

God "will give to each person according to what he has done." To those who by persistence in doing good seek glory, honor and immortality, he will give eternal life. But for those who are self-seeking and who reject the truth and follow evil, there will be wrath and anger. ...but glory, honor and peace for everyone who does good: first for the Jew, then for the Gentile. For God does not show favoritism. Romans 2: 6 – 8, 10 – 11

In these couple of versus we see that there is something we need to do. Be persistent by doing good, seeking glory, honor and immortality and we will be blessed with eternal life. See what Paul says about self seekers? Are we not that when we pass judgment? After all when we try to judge someone else, all we are really doing is trying to make ourselves feel better about ourselves. Thank God with me that He does not show favoritism; for we all have the opportunity for a reward of glory, honor, and peace.

But wait a minute; I thought that the way to salvation was simply faith in Jesus as the Holy Son of God and that he died for us on the cross? That there was nothing we can do to earn our salvation. Yes, that is correct, but we still have to live a life that honor and glorifies God the Father. Even Jesus did that. Look how Jesus prayed for himself in

John 17: 4 *"I have brought you glory on earth by completing the work you gave me to do."*

Jesus had work to do so why wouldn't we? Jesus came and shared the love and grace of God with all. Shouldn't that be our work also? Even to unbelievers? Yes even to unbelievers. This doesn't mean we allow the world to run over us, but it does mean that we humble ourselves and pray about uncomfortable situations. We cannot do this by ourselves. We need help and that help is God Himself by the gift of the Holy Spirit. But when we are self absorbed or self seeking, we actually will block out the Holy Spirit and his guidance. Trust me I know, for I have done this far too often. It is on my prayer list always that I would become less and that God will become greater in my life through His Holy Spirit.

Let's look at another of Jesus' teaching found in Matthew 25: 31 – 46 that demonstrates this. Here Jesus is telling us of what it will be like when he returns. Jesus says that all will be separated as a shepherd separates the sheep from the goats; sheep on the right and goats on the left. In essence the sheep will share in the glories of eternal life and the goats will be condemned to eternal punishment. What distinguishes them is what each person did to Jesus in their lifetime. Feed him when he was hungry, gave him a drink when he thirsted, invited him in even though he was a stranger, clothed him when he did not have enough clothes, took care of him when he was sick and visited him when he was in prison.

The fascinating thing about this teaching is, both the sheep and the goats ask when did we see you in these conditions. Jesus responded to both groups in the same manner:

"The King will reply, 'I tell you the truth, whatever you did for one of the least of these brothers of mine, you did for me." Vs 41 "He will reply, 'I tell you the truth, whatever you did not do for one of the least of these, you did not do for me." Vs 45

To the sheep (his true followers) he calls himself *"The King"*. To the goats he simply states *"He will reply"*.

Three very strong points jump out at me. First; many times in the New Testament it is pointed out that belief in Jesus is the only way to salvation and I agree with that. Here though Jesus clearly states that with salvation there must be some action to demonstrate that you are his. Second; both the sheep and the goats asked the same question. The sheep I believe ask because what they did to the least became a true second nature to them. They did not realize what their daily actions meant. It is not always about evangelizing through words, actions speak louder. The goats I believe ask because they did not realize how self absorbed they were, they never noticed the needs of others around them. Third; both groups refer to Jesus as "Lord" the sheep out of faith, love and joy that their King has arrived and the goats in an oh oh moment, they realized it was now to late.

What does this all mean? The answer is found in John 15: 17 *"This is my command: Love each other."* You might ask (as I did) I have to love? I just hate to love. It's just mushy and it does not fit my image, the world may make fun of me, it's not cool.

Well love is a requirement and a sign of being a Christian; of one that allows the Holy Spirit to work in him or her. Let's look again at something Paul wrote to the Galatians.

But the fruit of the Spirit is love, joy, peace, patience, kindness, goodness, faithfulness, gentleness and self-control. Against such things there is no law. Those who belong to Christ Jesus have crucified the sinful nature with its passions and desires. Since we live by the Spirit, let us keep in step with the Spirit. Let us not become conceited, provoking and envying each other. Galatians 5: 22 – 26

Okay, I can see some of these traits in some people and sometimes myself; but that love thing, that just gets me, and I am sure it gets a lot of people, besides its listed first. Does this mean I have to love first? Do I really have to love, even though I do not feel like loving anyone? Even though I have a hard time loving myself?

This brings me back to the original statements I made in the beginning of this chapter. I do not believe we are being taught what being a Christian is all about. I have heard some try, but it usually ends up what God can do for us. It also brings me to the point of this whole book. Let me make this clear, there are a lot of really good individual churches out there and there are some awesome individual Christians doing some amazing things for God, but it is not their doing it is God working through them. They just allowed themselves to be a vessel for God's grace. Yet overall I think that somehow we are still missing something. I will say it again, that I believe it is in the teaching.

We know that the disciples and apostles spent time teaching. I know this because of the New Testament letters. In these letters you find lots of teaching about so many daily issues and how to deal with them as Christians. This tells me that when you accept Jesus as your Savior there is no sudden change, you are still the same person as before, except now you are saved. There is a process in the life change and the thought pattern change. Romans 12: 2 states this: *Do not conform any longer to the pattern of this world, but be transformed by the renewing of your mind.* This is a strong indication that the process of becoming a Christian is just that, a process. We are to be transformed how? Only by the renewing of our mind. How do we do that? By spending time with God, learning His word, learning His way, it is a process that is repeated daily as long as we are on this earth.

Look at the disciples. They spent three years following Jesus and were with him almost twenty-four hours, seven days a week. They saw Jesus heal hundreds maybe thousands of people. They saw him feed five thousand men not counting the women and children, yet a little while later they are faced with four thousand men (plus women and children) that are hungry and they ask Jesus where they can get enough bread to feed them. The disciples see the compassion of Jesus always putting others first, yet at the end of the time with him they argued who would be greater in the kingdom. Change does not come easy. We fight the whole time because we are selfish creatures at heart.

But this still leaves the question: How should we go about teaching about love and loving your neighbor as yourself? The answer of course is to allow God to teach us through His word. In God's infinite wisdom, I believe He knew we would have a hard time with this so he gave us the answer in clear black and white. It is found in His word and written by Peter of all people. Remember Peter? The same Peter that was bold enough to jump out of the boat to walk on water, only to lose his focus and sink. Peter selfish enough that told Jesus he must not go to the cross. Peter bold enough to chop an ear off a servant at the garden when Jesus was betrayed. Peter who said that he would die along with Jesus, would never deny him, only to angrily deny that he knew Jesus a few hours later.

Yet this same Peter was the one that stood up in front of thousands on Pentecost to deliver a powerful sermon about Jesus and what the Jews and Romans did to him. This Peter, the common fisherman became so eloquent as he taught and wrote. This only goes to show that yes Jesus takes us that are simple and makes a strong tool out of us. And yes it does take a period of learning, transforming and all of this is provided by the gift of the Holy Spirit.

Other readings for study:

Look up some of the people that Jesus healed in the gospels. Matthew 25: 31 - 46

Chapter 5

Stepping Stones

My suffering was good for me, for it taught me to pay attention to your decrees. Psalm 119: 71 (NLT)

Like I said, I grew up in a Christian home, went to a Christian elementary school and to a Christian high school. I saw many things that I did not think were very Christian like, (lack of grace, love, compassion), because of this I felt like I was driven from the church in the mid to late seventy's. I went back to church in the early eighty's only to see behavior again that was very un-Christian like. So I felt that once again I was driven away. In actuality, I was running away from truth. A truth that tells me, we are all fallen and guilty of sin, therefore violating God's decrees. A truth that tells me that because we are all fallen, we are all subject to make mistakes and are in need of God's grace in order to make it to eternity. A truth that tells me we are definitely missing something in our teaching.

I stayed away from church but never really gave up on God; however I did not live the way God wanted me to. During this period I always felt a tugging at my heart, like I was missing something. Then one day in 1995 I was pulled into a church after arguing with God for a long time. I started going regularly, recommitted my life to God, then the following year my wife Sandy also started going to church with me. Sandy submitted her life to Jesus and was baptized in

1999. Sandy had gone to church when she was a child but was terrified by the style of preaching she was submitted to, so she gave up on it at a very early age.

It was in 1999 that I went through a trial that tested me in every way. A trial that attacked my thought process, my faith and my relationship with Sandy. Notice this attack came after Sandy's baptism. Satan has a way of trying to bring us down when God is bringing us up. (See the temptation of Jesus in the desert. This came right after John the Baptist baptized Jesus. Matthew 3: 13 – 17 & 4: 1 – 11.) Yet it was in this trial that God gently guided me into his truth and allowed me to see that I did not know anything about love. As I was discovering this, God brought me to the Peter's writing that guided me to the truth of love.

The truth about love is that it really is a process. When you see a lack of Christian love in your community; you do not learn a whole lot from that community. Sure I had a lot of love in my family, but that is to be expected. Isn't it? This trial I went through made me question everything I had done and learned in my life. It made me revisit every opinion I had formed. It was clear that my entire life was spent running away from God and his grace and everything else that was good in my life. So God brought me to this process in clear black and white in his word. I believe God is directing me to write this book as another learning tool. Yes I confess, I am in need of being reminded. I think I did not let other people help me and I did not offer to help them as much as I should have. Maybe also I can help others through the haze. This haze is one that is brought about by our selfishness, just as mine was. One that thinks I know best and what the church is doing doesn't meet my expectations.

Imagine you are walking a wide path along a river. This river is life that is passing you by. The path you are on, even though it is wide, is very difficult to walk on because there are a lot of people on this same path crowding you out trying to get ahead of you. There are lots of holes and roots that cause you to stumble, jagged rocks that cut and bruise when you fall and the path is a constant up and down and very winding. There are thorn bushes every where you look. You try to avoid one, only to get tangled up in another. People shove you down and it seems like you just can't get your balance. You have to keep zigzagging to try and stay on level ground; but it is difficult. Sometimes it seems like you are going in circles. On the other side of the river you see a path going in the same direction. You see that

Step Stones

the path is very narrow but it looks like it is straight from where you are it appears to be a much easier walk than what you are on now. There are far less people on that path, and if you look closely they look like they are helping each other down the path. Everything on the other side even appears to be brighter, clearer, and somehow almost peaceful. It feels so right to get to the other side. You decide to check it out further and you walk along the bank wondering how you are going to get there; looking for every possible crossing, even contemplating wading across but the current is too fast, too cold and the water is too deep. You keep walking upstream then down stream, yet you find no way to cross. You walk past a bend in the river and suddenly you see the way. You run to the spot, and then come to a stop. The way across looks a little hazardous and you think to yourself that maybe this path

Step Stones

on this side is not so bad after all. You look back but you know you got to get to the other side because that is where this other path is; besides the path you were on really was miserable. You stand there and contemplate how you are going to do this, but the longer you stand there, the more hazardous it looks. You hear a voice inside telling you to come on, it will be okay, but you stand there waiting, thinking. You hear another voice inside telling you to turn around and get back, stay on this side, that you can do it alone. But you know that you just can't do it anymore by yourself. You need help.

What is this way across? There are seven stones, eight if you count the last one that is three quarters in the water and one quarter on the bank. The stones are sitting in the current just above the water line. Each stone is just about the right size for you to get one foot on maybe the edge of your second foot if you balance just right.

The first stone will take a leap to get to, if you miss you could slip and fall, and face the possibility of being swept away in the cold water. The second stone is real close to the first, almost close enough that you could stand on both at the same time. The third stone looks a little larger where you could rest and let your heart calm, but it is in a little deeper water also. The fourth stone will take a short jump to get to and it looks a little shaky. Then you look at the fifth stone sitting in the deepest part of the current. It is very small and looks like it is wet and rounded from the current flowing over it and it will take a good jump to get to that one. The reward is the sixth and seventh stones are mere steps apart and look very solid in the water. Then there is the last one right on the bank and it looks like it is a solid rock and leads right onto the path you want to be on.

I know that God led me to this crossing and some incredible opportunities and learning's. I still sometimes feel that I am stuck on one of them and at other times I feel that I am standing on the last stone just looking behind where I came from, afraid to move any further. But those are just feelings, attacks, and not the truth. The truth is God would not have allowed me to come to this crossing if he would not help me get across. What I do know is that I have made it across and now the feelings I get are feelings of insecurity which I only get when I try to do things on my own. I am still learning that as I walk the narrow path I need to keep looking forward keeping my focus on God; He brought me to this point.

So what is this set of stepping stones?

For this very reason, make every effort to add to your faith goodness; and to goodness, knowledge; and to knowledge, self-control; and to self-control, perseverance; and to perseverance, godliness; and to godliness, brotherly kindness; and to brotherly kindness, love. 2 Peter 1: 5 – 7

See the step stones? The rest of this book will be devoted to each of these step stones. I intend to take us on my journey, looking to God's word to help us grow into God's grace, which ultimately calls us to share that same grace to all no matter what the circumstances.

Other readings for study:
    Psalm 19, Philippians 1: 9 – 11, Philippians 3: 12 - 16

Chapter 6

Faith

Now faith is being sure of what we hope for and certain of what we do not see. Hebrews 11: 1

I just got up from my computer desk, went to the kitchen and got a cup of coffee. When I came back, I stood in front of my desk with my back to the chair. I at this point cannot see my chair yet I sit down anyway. I know the chair is there. That is faith in the very simplest of terms.

However, I do not believe that is the kind of faith the writer of Hebrews had in mind when he wrote the above. What I described is probably a better definition of common sense. Following are some key scripture verses that will walk us through the basics of faith.

In the beginning God created the heavens and the earth. Genesis 1:1

So God created man in his own image, in the image of God he created him; male and female he created them. Genesis 1: 27

For since the creation of the world God's invisible qualities—his eternal power and divine nature—have been clearly seen, being understood from what has been made, so that men are without excuse. For although they knew God, they neither glorified him as God nor gave thanks to him, but their thinking became futile and their foolish hearts were darkened. Although they claimed to be wise, they became fools and exchanged the glory of the immortal God for images made to look like mortal man and birds and animals and reptiles. Therefore God gave them over in the sinful desires of their hearts to sexual impurity for the degrading of their bodies with one another. They exchanged the truth of God for a lie, and worshiped and served created things rather than the Creator—who is forever praised. Amen. Romans 1: 20 – 25

There is no one righteous, not even one. Romans 3: 6b

In the beginning was the Word (Jesus), and the Word was with God, and the Word was God. He was with God in the beginning. Through him all things were made; without him nothing was made that has been made. In him was life, and that life was the light of men. The light shines in the darkness, but the darkness has not understood it. John 1: 1 – 5

Jesus answered, "I am the way and the truth and the life. No one comes to the Father except through me. If you really knew me, you would know my Father as well. From now on, you do know him and have seen him." John 14: 6 – 7

Simon Peter answered, "You are the Christ, the Son of the living God." Matthew 16: 16

Carrying his own cross, he went out to the place of the Skull (which in Aramaic is called Golgotha). Here they crucified him, John 19: 17 – 18a

Jesus said, "It is finished." With that, he bowed his head and gave up his spirit. John 19: 30b

So Joseph bought some linen cloth, took down the body, wrapped it in the linen, and placed it in a tomb cut out of rock. Then he rolled a stone against the entrance of the tomb. Mark 15: 46

Don't be alarmed," he said. "You are looking for Jesus the Nazarene, who was crucified. He has risen! Mark 16: 6

Then Jesus came to them and said, "All authority in heaven and on earth has been given to me. Therefore go and make disciples of all nations, baptizing them in the name of the Father and of the Son and of the Holy Spirit, and teaching them to obey everything I have commanded you. And surely I am with you always, to the very end of the age." Matthew 28: 18 – 20

After his suffering, he showed himself to these men and gave many convincing proofs that he was alive. He appeared to them over a period of forty days and spoke about the kingdom of God. Acts 1: 3

He was taken up before their very eyes, and a cloud hid him from their sight. They were looking intently up into the sky as he was going, when suddenly two men dressed in white stood beside them. "Men of Galilee," they said, "why do you stand here looking into the sky? This same Jesus, who has been taken from you into heaven, will come back in the same way you have seen him go into heaven." Acts 1: 9b – 11

Brothers, we do not want you to be ignorant about those who fall asleep, or to grieve like the rest of men, who have no hope. We believe that Jesus died and rose again and so we believe that God will bring with Jesus those who have fallen asleep in him. According to the Lord's own word, we tell you that we who are still alive, who are left till the coming of the Lord, will certainly not precede those who have fallen asleep. For the Lord himself will come down from heaven, with a loud command, with the voice of the archangel and with the trumpet call of God, and the dead in Christ will rise first. After that, we who are still alive and are left will be caught up together with them in the clouds to meet the Lord in the air. And so we will be with the Lord forever. Therefore encourage each other with these words. 1 Thessalonians 4: 13 – 18

Just wait a minute here. These things have been said over and over again for two thousand years. How come Jesus has not returned yet? How much more can go on? If there really is a God how come there is war? Cancer? Poverty? Why was my father taken from me when I was ten years old and left my mother fighting to support us? Why did the church community turn their backs on us so often? Turn their backs on me?

All valid questions, are they not? I have had all of these questions and many more. The world wants to keep throwing these things out at me to try and confuse me, to make me doubt. Yet when I look at all these questions they are centered on one thing and one thing only. Me!

I look at these things and want answers. I want answers from God, for Him to explain to me why these things are occurring.

"For my thoughts are not your thoughts, neither are your ways my ways," declares the LORD. Isaiah 55: 8

It is pretty selfish of me to demand answers to the God that created the entire universe. For there was not one thing ever created that God did not have His hand in. When I look at the scripture verses that outline the tenets of faith, I can see a plan. A plan that has been carried out to the tiniest detail over thousands of years by a perfect and gracious God, who desires a close personal relationship with me and with each and every one of us, His creation.

Yet I try to insist that it is all about me and I fear. The path across the river looks easier than the one I am on yet there are not many people over there. I see a few people that I know, but there are many more that I know on this side. Many glance over to the other side, many stop and look but not many are even thinking about what I am; that is taking that first step to the stone of faith. I wonder what is going on that so many can see the path but do not take it. Is this crossing of step stones the only way across? It seems like I have spent a life time trying to find a better path, but I am afraid. Even though it is hard on this side, it is what I know. There are some people on the other side encouraging me to jump to the first stone of faith. But I do not know. So I stand here wondering and thinking about what I have seen in the past. Fear comes over me, then after much thought a feeling of peace.

I look down and yes this first stone will take a good leap to get to, but I decide to try it. After all, the water around the stone does not look too deep. If I slip it appears to be only a few inches deep, but it is swift and cold. My mind immediately brings this thought up, if I slip and fall backwards or sideways

Step Stones

I might get washed down stream. As I stand there I look back and see the others on this side, on this path that I was just on. They look happy yet when I look into their eyes I see despair; the same despair that I feel. There is something better, there has to be. I stand there thinking and I look down at my feet. Unbeknownst to me, I have stood there long enough many have passed by me. Most staying on the path on this side, a few have jumped past me to the first stone and kept on going to where I want to go.

I have stood there so long I have started to sink into the mud. Have you ever stood on a beach and as the water lapped at your feet the sand slowly turned watery and your feet disappear into the soft sand? I decide I have to do something. Either turn around and take the path I was on, or take that leap to the first stone of faith.

For God so loved the world that he gave his one and only Son, that whoever believes in him shall not perish but have eternal life. For God did not send his Son into the world to condemn the world, but to save the world through him. John 3: 16 – 17

I hear this scripture and turn my head to see who is speaking this to me. I realize the voice is in my head, in my heart. The voice is asking me if I believe that; I say I do. The voice is asking me if I want to have eternal life or death. I answer that I want life. The voice asks me what I am waiting for. I respond by saying that I have been around the church for many years and I have not seen what I thought it should have been. The voice tells me that I am being foolish by basing my destiny upon others, that even though others have harmed me, it is no excuse. (It's funny that my mother has been saying the same thing to me for years.) The voice tells me that I am floundering in my sinful desires and in my nature. That this nature can be changed if I wish. I argue again that this life is hard but if I go to church there will be guilt and condemnation added to my already full spinning out of control life.

Those who live according to the sinful nature have their minds set on what that nature desires; Romans 8: 5a

I realize that yes, I have been living to my desires and have become trapped by them. The world for the last twenty-five years or more has been bombarding me with the suggestions that I need to do what feels right. They say there is no right or wrong just whatever feels good. The world also has told me that there is more than one path, but I've spent some time looking and never found anything else.

So here I stand with my feet sinking in the muddy mire. I actually jump to the first stone, only to jump back because of fear. The thought comes over me that I have been here at this very spot for most of those twenty-five years since I felt like I was driven from the church because I didn't meet their expectations. This river was life, passing me by.

The voice I hear tells me that I have actually jumped back and forth to the first stone of faith and the muddy shore several times now. The voice tells me that I would always jump back because the stone felt wobbly to me, that I was in reality being selfish and wanted to live my life my way. The voice says that the reason it did was because I was trying to balance and achieve salvation on my own. I didn't want to rely on anyone, not even God because of my fears.

I scream out and cry out because I know that to be the truth. I have tried on my own because what I was taught as a kid, I rarely saw in action. I tried on my own because I have been alone for so long now. Yes I have been married, yes I have family and friends; but I have been alone within myself. I cry out again; this time to the Lord!

To you, O LORD, I called; to the Lord I cried for mercy: Hear, O LORD, and be merciful to me; O LORD, be my help." Psalms 30: 8 & 10

There I did it and took that leap again, this time though, the stone felt solid, not shaky like before. I thought the jump would be difficult because my feet were planted on the mud and mire and it was starting to feel slimy and the water was starting to rush around them. When I landed on that stone I almost out of instinct jumped back to the muddy bank, but this time I kept my eyes on the Lord; on my new desire, my new commitment.

He lifted me out of the slimy pit, out of the mud and mire; he set my feet on a rock and gave me a firm place to stand. Psalm 40: 2

This stone of faith is a little firmer than it first looked like. I am feeling better about my decision to take that leap. Now what do I do? Where do I go from here? I look to the Lord for he is the one who helped me across that first leap to the stone of faith.

With that leap, I for the first time sincerely accepted Jesus as my savior and the truth that he paid my price for my sinful ways. Because of that I can say with David as he wrote these words:

Hide your face from my sins and blot out all my iniquity. Create in me a pure heart, O God, and renew a steadfast spirit within me. Psalms 51: 9 – 10

I can rejoice for the forgiveness of my sins, knowing now that the Lord will help me in my struggles of life. The voice I heard, I realize was the Holy Spirit of God. This same Spirit was promised to us by Jesus to be our comforter and our guide.

I stand there on that stone of faith thinking that my entire life I believed in God; yet I never trusted him, never had the faith to trust Him. I hear the Holy Spirit tell me that it is okay to stand there and get my bearings, but I should not look back. I stand thinking about faith and what it really is.

Therefore, there is now no condemnation for those who are in Christ Jesus, because through Christ Jesus the law of the Spirit of life set me free from the law of sin and death. For what the law was powerless to do in that it was weakened by the sinful nature, God did by sending his own Son in the likeness of sinful man to be a sin offering. Romans 8: 1 – 3a

I feel some peace in my life for the first time since I can't remember when. I have just experienced the grace of God. God's grace is a gift lovingly and freely given to us, even though we have done nothing to earn it.

I still hear other voices calling to me from the bank I just left. These voices are telling me to come back, that there is more fun on this side. I refuse to listen but instead look forward and hear the voices of scripture telling me about faith. The most remarkable thing I learn is that God is the one who is faithful. He is faithful to His word, His promises and there is nothing I can do to change that. I can't add to it or take away from it. I realize that because of God's great faithfulness and His amazing grace, faith is really not that big of a leap after all.

For every child of God defeats this evil world, and we achieve this victory through our faith. 1 John 5: 4 NLT

Step Stones

With victory in hand I stand there thinking about that next step. It too looks a little shaky and unfamiliar to me; fear again begins to grip me. I wonder what should be done next, so I look to what Jesus himself said about this.

I have told you these things, so that in me you may have peace. John 16: 33a

I feel the peace so I have a little confidence now and look to the next stone of goodness. When I looked at it from the bank it looked a little smaller than it actually is and a little further. Now that I am here it is closer and I believe that I can step to it and stand on it at the same time I stand on the stone of faith.

Other readings for study:

Psalm 19, Amos 4: 13, Hebrews 11, 2 Corinthians 6: 1- 2, Romans 1
Just a thought: Faith is a relationship with God; one that must be lived, not just learned. That was my mistake from the beginning; I learned it, but did not live it. Faith cannot be taught by words alone, it must have demonstrations; sheep and goats.

Chapter 7

Goodness

The LORD is good to all; he has compassion on all he has made. Psalm 145: 9

I pay particular attention to this verse from the Psalms. It states that the Lord is good to whom? To all! To whom does He have compassion on? Again to all! It does not say that God only loves those that have given their life to Him, or to those who follow certain rules, or have a certain income level or dress a certain way, go to a certain church etc. No, He is God of all creation, and He loves all of it, and all of us.

So now that I have been standing on this first stone of faith, I feel this desire to take the next step. I put my foot out and measure the right distance and there I did it. I have one foot on the second stone of goodness and I still have the other foot on faith.

I think about it a little and decide for me to understand real goodness; it will take the balance of faith to get started. I agree with the voice within me that if God can be good to all even though many of the all will deny Him, then I have a responsibility to do the same. After all Paul tells us this:

We are therefore Christ's ambassadors, as though God were making his appeal through us. 2 Corinthians 5: 20a

When you see this, you just know in your heart that this is an appeal for genuine goodness in truth, not just an outward appearance of goodness. It is not just common courtesy or doing it because it is "the right thing" to do. No, it must come from the heart and be free flowing and natural. I have seen many people, including myself treat people with goodness, only to talk bad about them as soon as they leave the room or have left the scene. I live in the Nashville, Tennessee region and there is a popular saying around here and it may go into other parts of the south I just do not know. When I first moved here I heard many people say with a look of compassion or a small smile "Oh bless your heart". People would use this term directly to someone else's face when they were explaining something that went wrong in their lives. It could be something simple like a traffic ticket or greater like an illness and everything in-between. At first I thought that these people around here, which is known as the buckle to the Bible belt, really were good people full of compassion. You can imagine my shock when after a couple of years I come to find out what the real meaning of this statement is. Are you ready for it? It means "Oh you are so stupid". Now granted at times I believe it is used in the good sense, but many times it is used in a derogatory way, it is hard to tell. It is just another way for people to try and make themselves feel like they are better than others. This is just a selfish act.

With their mouths they bless, but in their hearts they curse Psalms 62: 4b

This should not happen, especially coming from the mouths of Christians. Read again what Paul wrote. We are (Christians, followers of Jesus) the ambassadors of Christ. God is making an appeal to those that are not Christian through us. What damage does it do when you see Christians demeaning others to make themselves feel better? How many people have been driven from the church because of this sort of behavior? I know that was one of the reasons I left.

Jesus said that we are to go into the world and be salt and light; which tells me that there is a responsibility that goes with being a follower of Christ.

I am the vine; you are the branches. If a man remains in me and I in him, he will bear much fruit; apart from me you can do nothing. John 15: 5

Jesus is the vine we are the branches and what are we to do? Bear much fruit. How do we do this? By being the salt and the light, we now represent Jesus himself.

Standing with one foot on the step stone of faith and the other on the step stone of goodness I recall a teaching about Jesus name. Most people will pray and finish their prayers "in Jesus name". Many people think that prayers will not be answered unless you finish this way. Many (mostly non-Christians) will say I prayed and didn't get what I wanted as if "in Jesus name" is the magic word. In all actuality to pray in Jesus name you must first live in Jesus name.

Here is an example: There is a small country town with a small produce market in it. The owners of the market, lets call them Bob and Martha are very generous people. People are always coming in to buy some fresh produce, and because of the tough economy around this town some of the people do not have very much money. So Bob and Martha in an effort to help will give produce away to people that are struggling, just to make sure they are getting something to eat. On occasion Bob and Martha will call down to the grocery store and make arrangements with the grocery store owner to give them some groceries, that Bob and Martha will pay for later or as is usually the case pay for it in trade with some fresh produce from their farm. The grocery store owner will in turn give the struggling people some canned goods, bread and some milk. The people are going to the store to receive something in Bob and Martha's name. Almost all of the time those that received help will come back and try to pay for their goods or work it off in some manner. All are very grateful.

Now there is someone that tries to take advantage of Bob and Martha's name and goes to the grocery store and loads up their cart with groceries of all kinds including lots of expensive meats. This person then goes to the checkout counter and after all is totaled, several hundred dollars worth, they say that Bob and Martha told them to come and do this. The owner of the store tells them that they must pay or leave without the food. Why did the owner of the grocery store say this? Because he knew Bob and Martha and what they do for those they try to help. This person did not act in the way that all the others do when they get sent there by Bob and Martha. They tried to take advantage of the good nature of Bob and Martha. They tried to dishonor Bob and Martha's name.

This is the same for us when we say we are a follower of Christ but do not act in a manner that honors his name. In our example Bob and Martha chose the ones they wanted to help. This person tried to make himself chosen.

You did not choose me, but I chose you and appointed you to go and bear fruit—fruit that will last. Then the Father will give you whatever you ask in my name. John 15: 16

Jesus came into this world and bore fruit to the glory of Father God. In all he did, Jesus did to glorify the name of his Father. Since we are now followers of Jesus we too must bear that same fruit by living the way Jesus did. Jesus was good to all men, even the ones that disagreed with him and the ones that put him on trial and crucified him. In all this he did not sin. So we too must work to do the same; not in our strength but in God's.

Think about this for a minute. If we have faith but do not exercise it in our life, what good is it? If we have faith and still treat other people as beneath us, what good is it? If we have faith and try to get our selfish way all the time, what good is it? Let's look at what James says:

What good is it, my brothers, if a man claims to have faith but has no deeds? Can such faith save him? Suppose a brother or sister is without clothes and daily food. If one of you says to him, "Go, I wish you well; keep warm and well fed," but does nothing about his physical needs, what good is it? In the same way, faith by itself, if it is not accompanied by action, is dead. But someone will say, "You have faith; I have deeds." Show me your faith without deeds, and I will show you my faith by what I do. You believe that there is one God. Good! Even the demons believe that—and shudder. James 2: 14 – 19

So here I am standing on both step stones at the same time. I lift my foot off of the faith stone and stand squarely on the step stone of goodness. I realize as I did this, my faith grew stronger and stayed with me. I also realize that this goodness is a little more difficult than I anticipated. You see our selfish nature just wants to get in the way. So in order to practice this goodness, it takes a lot of faith, patience, and prayer. With my life starting to change; my attitudes are changing, as is my talk. Those that I know are seeing the change, some like it and others try to get me to come back to the river bank were I just came from. The struggles of my inner self are getting tougher.

I learn that the goodness we are talking about here can really be translated from the Greek as virtue. Virtue has an upstanding quality to it. It means to be commendable in all you do. This means to give your best effort at work, at home with your familial relationships whether that is your wife, husband, children, parents, brothers, sisters, and actually everyone you come in contact with. It means to show common courtesy to strangers, returning a smile with a smile not a sneer. Helping others with simple things like opening a door for them, letting them go first. All of these traits used to be quite common but has become more and more scarce in the last few decades. It brings to mind another of Jesus teachings. It goes like this.

Jesus called them together and said, "You know that the rulers of the Gentiles lord it over them, and their high officials exercise authority over them. Not so with you. Instead, whoever wants to become great among you must be your servant, and whoever wants to be first must be your slave just as the Son of Man did not come to be served, but to serve, and to give his life as a ransom for many." Matthew 20: 25 - 28

In a nutshell, to be a follower of Jesus and to practice the goodness that Peter wrote about and saw first hand, I must put others first. That goes in direct conflict with what the world likes to teach and act. It is extremely hard to put my desires and wants to the side and see to it that others around me are taken care of.

As I practice this, I realize that there are blessings in this. When God sees that we are generous (not necessarily monetarily), but in our actions, God will generously bless us in more ways than we can imagine. Again it does not necessarily mean blessings in a monetary or possession's fashion. I insert this notion of a monetary basis because I know some will automatically assume an advance in their net worth when they think of blessings in abundance.

Paul wrote to Timothy some vital instructions that apply to me also. Paul is instructing Timothy on how to teach the new believers and since I am fairly new at this, it most definitely applies to me.

Command them to do good, to be rich in good deeds, and to be generous and willing to share. 1 Timothy 6: 18

Basically this means that I need to change my way of thinking. The old way wants to be selfish and be of a receiving nature instead of having a generous nature. Remember that God gave to me extremely generously by giving me salvation for calling on Jesus as my Savior and acknowledged that Jesus is the Son of God. Who gave of his life so generously to all. See John 3: 16 – 17

So from now on we regard no one from a worldly point of view. Though we once regarded Christ in this way, we do so no longer. Therefore, if anyone is in Christ, he is a new creation; the old has gone, the new has come! 2 Corinthians 5: 16 - 17

So here I stand on the step stone of goodness and after some time realizing I am a new creation, I feel some tugging in my heart. This tugging seems to be a relationship growing; a relationship with God. It is a trust that goes beyond faith and is more than just being good, it's as if I need to know more. I look down and ahead to see the next step stone. This one is close and larger, but also very familiar. I have been taught about God most of my life. It is as if I had somehow jumped to this stone before I had the faith. Maybe it was one of the paths I had been on before when I was searching. I hesitate, this stone is in deeper water but I also notice the stone has a solid base to it. It is the step stone of knowledge.

Other readings for study:

Psalms 19, Luke 3: 7 - 8a, Ephesians 2: 8 – 10, 1 Timothy 6: 11 - 20

Chapter 8

Knowledge

For the LORD gives wisdom, and from his mouth come knowledge and understanding. He holds victory in store for the upright, he is a shield to those whose walk is blameless, for he guards the course of the just and protects the way of his faithful ones. Then you will understand what is right and just and fair—every good path. For wisdom will enter your heart, and knowledge will be pleasant to your soul. Proverbs 2: 6 - 10

The knowledge that Peter was referring to is not the knowledge of worldly things. I guess in their own way they hold some importance in our lives, but they should not take precedence over the knowledge of God and His ways. Paul tells the Corinthians the following:

Do not deceive yourselves. If any one of you thinks he is wise by the standards of this age, he should become a "fool" so that he may become wise. For the wisdom of this world is foolishness in God's sight. As it is written: "He catches the wise in their craftiness" and again, "The Lord knows that the thoughts of the wise are futile." So then, no more boasting about men! 1 Corinthians 3: 18 – 21a

Just to make my point about worldly knowledge and knowledge of the Lord, let's go back to a time long ago; several thousand years to be exact. To the time of Solomon who became the wisest man on the face of the earth. One just needs to read Proverbs, The Song of Solomon and Ecclesiastes to see the wisdom that this King of Israel had. Just a quick read through 1 Kings chapter three, you see Solomon as a young King asking God for a discerning heart so that he could carry out justice. God not only answered this request, but blessed him with even more. God told Solomon that he would give him a wise and discerning heart so that no man will be wiser than him, then or ever. God also granted Solomon things he did not ask for, riches and honor, so that there would be no equal among men. Then God threw this in, that if Solomon walked in the ways of the Lord he would also have a long life.

Now one just needs to read the books mentioned above to see how wise and knowledgeable Solomon was. He wrote things that get us to do some serious deep thinking today. He wrote about subjects that plague us today. See Ecclesiastes and Solomon's struggles with what he saw people struggling for. He came to the conclusion that it is good to be merry and enjoy the day. No need for stressing out in this lifetime. Solomon came to the conclusion that all things are useless unless you serve the Lord God your creator. Look at these words of his.

Now all has been heard; here is the conclusion of the matter: Fear God and keep his commandments, for this is the whole duty of man. For God will bring every deed into judgment, including every hidden thing, whether it is good or evil. Ecclesiastes 12: 13 – 14

I like most people did not like to hear those words; God will bring everything into judgment. Oh sure they can say things like "that is only if you believe in God" or "I don't want to serve a God like that", but it does not matter what we think. The truth is we will be brought into judgment even if you "feel" like you are a good person or have "lived" a good life. Unless you declare that Jesus is the Son of God and that he is your personal savior, you will be judged not to your liking. Only those who accept Jesus as your personal savior are going to be judged in a most magnificent manner – eternal life.

Now back to my original thought process.

Solomon in all his wisdom, riches, honor and knowledge had one terrible flaw; himself. He got caught up in his love for women and so doing, defied the commands of God.

King Solomon, however, loved many foreign women besides 1 Kings 11: 1a

So Solomon did evil in the eyes of the LORD; he did not follow the LORD completely, as David his father had done. 1 Kings 11: 6

Although he had forbidden Solomon to follow other gods, Solomon did not keep the LORD's command. So the LORD said to Solomon, "Since this is your attitude and you have not kept my covenant and my decrees, which I commanded you, I will most certainly tear the kingdom away from you and give it to one of your subordinates. Nevertheless, for the sake of David your father, I will not do it during your lifetime. I will tear it out of the hand of your son. Yet I will not tear the whole kingdom from him, but will give him one tribe for the sake of David my servant and for the sake of Jerusalem, which I have chosen." 1 Kings 11: 10 -13

So, if even Solomon failed, where can I find this knowledge? Here I am standing on the step stone of goodness and wanting to take that step onto the stone of knowledge; but how do I do that? Look back to the verse from Ecclesiastes 12. "Fear the Lord and keep His commandments."

I tell myself to go ahead and take that step. Now I need to start digging into the word of God, The Holy Bible. I need to read daily His word and find not only guidance for this life, but preparation for things I currently feel unprepared for, no matter what the situation may be.

Paul tells us in his first letter to the Corinthians that we have the Spirit of God living in us since we committed our lives to Him.

We have not received the spirit of the world but the Spirit who is from God, that we may understand what God has freely given us. This is what we speak, not in words taught us by human wisdom but in words taught by the Spirit, expressing spiritual truths in spiritual words. 1 Corinthians 2: 12 - 13

The spiritual man makes judgments about all things, but he himself is not subject to any man's judgment: "For who has known the mind of the Lord that he may instruct him?" But we have the mind of Christ. 1 Corinthians 2: 15 -16

I found that the key is to keep pressing on, striving for more each day. God is always with us in the form of His Holy Spirit, it is up to us to make sure that relationship develops into the very best it can be. I can do this by allowing the Holy Spirit to work in me. The key word is allowing.

I found out that I do not have to be smart, strong, good looking or rich. God wants me to come to him in humble submission and when I do that, hold on and actively search for the wonders of God. Since I took that first step onto the step stone of faith I have become new.

Since you have taken off your old self with its practices and have put on the new self, which is being renewed in knowledge in the image of its Creator. Colossians 3: 9b – 10

I have seen some incredible things from those you would least expect it. People that could barely hold a conversation when talking about general things; but could recall scripture in an eloquent manner. People that were shy and introverted stand up and speak as if they gave speeches every day of their life. People that only have a few years of education teach in ways that makes your heart leap with joy. There are countless examples and all are brought to us by the Spirit of God within them.

It is also at this point where I began to realize that yes there is a relationship with God through Jesus Christ and the Holy Spirit within me. When I first took that leap of faith I felt like there was a special joy within me. Something had definitely changed but I was not sure.

Then when I did take that next step of goodness, consciously and many times subconsciously being nicer to those around me, even the ones I loved, I felt like I had a different set of values and that there was something genuinely changing about myself. I felt like there was always somebody with me as I went. My relationship with the Lord was starting to develop in ways I had no idea of.

Now I stand on this step stone of knowledge and as I start to learn more and more of the Lord, there is strong feelings that yes the Holy Spirit is at work in me. It is at this point also where many attacks of the flesh and of the world will become evident. A word of caution here; the attacks of Satan come in form that makes you question what you are learning now, and trying to make you compare them with what you learned from the world before. I know that if I was not careful, I would stumble and fall off of this step-stone. I had to diligently seek the Lord in prayer and in His word. I could read something from the Bible, and all of my worldly knowledge will say that is not what I learned before. Yet somehow I knew that the world is wrong and what I just read is correct. Seeking the wisdom and knowledge of others helped me through this. I listened to many Preachers and Pastors on the radio and television. I read countless books to help me gain the knowledge I now have.

However I really owe all the credit to the Lord himself; guiding me through His Holy Spirit, showing me what was truth and what was not. If what I heard and read did not match with God's word; I put that to the side. Oh, I still used that in my knowledge base. I just now used it to recognize the untruth that is so abundant in this world. It equipped me in a different manner.

All Scripture is God-breathed and is useful for teaching, rebuking, correcting and training in righteousness, so that the man of God may be thoroughly equipped for every good work. 2 Timothy 3: 16 -1 7

I read this and just know that it is God working within me. A feeling of peace and joy that is different than when I first believed started developing. I see that God is with me, helping me to do the good work that the step of goodness wanted to bring out of me. Yet somehow, I get the feeling that this relationship that I am developing did not originate with me, no it started with God and that he was looking for me. Maybe the better term is, He was waiting for me.

When I consider your heavens, the work of your fingers, the moon and the stars, which you have set in place, what is man that you are mindful of him, the son of man that you care for him? Psalm 8: 3 -4

With this relationship being developed, I understand that the reason that God sent Jesus to die for the world was so that the original intent of creating man could be restored. God wants to be with us and to share the riches of His knowledge with us.

I have called you friends, for everything that I learned from my Father I have made known to you. John 15: 15b

Solomon had the faith as expressed when he asked the Lord for wisdom to help him rule the kingdom of Israel. He had the goodness because if you read his story as found in 1 Kings he was generous to the people, in his building of the temple and with his dealings with other Kings and rulers of other nations. He most definitely had the knowledge but he failed in the next step of our step stone path though the river of life; which is self-control.

Other readings for study:

Proverbs, Words of Jesus found in Matthew 5 – 7,

Chapter 9

Self-Control

Be self-controlled and alert. Your enemy the devil prowls around like a roaring lion looking for someone to devour. I Peter 5: 8

Here I am, standing on the step stone of knowledge, having taken the initial step of faith, to the step of goodness, and now to the step of knowledge. I look ahead and see a stone that looks small, like it would be hard to balance on. Water sometimes slaps at the stone making it wet and slippery, with moss gathered on the edges. Do I dare take that step? It looks like it will take a small jump and if I land to the side; most likely I will slip and fall into the river running the risk of being swept away.

I draw faith, from my first leap. I look at the blessings from God that He graciously shared with me in abundance from my stay on the stone of goodness. Now with the strength I have from the stone of knowledge, I decide that my relationship with God has developed to the point that I gain courage enough to jump onto the stone of self-control.

But wait a minute! What is this self-control that we are talking about? What do I have to do? Greater fear starts to take over my thinking. Old emotions start to creep back into my thought patterns. My mind starts to wander and race, going back to things I did in the past, laughing at the fun that I had (many times at the expense of someone else and their feelings). I ask if I get on this step stone of self control will I turn into some other person I am not. Voices from my past call out to me to come back to the river bank I just came from. These voices tell me that what I have just experienced on the step stones of faith, goodness and knowledge were just a little sidetrack in my life. These voices tell me that there is no such thing as salvation for me because I did too much. That there will be too much required of me, and for that, I have no hope. These voices are getting louder and I start to think that maybe these voices are right, that I am not able to be saved.

I pause to shake these voices away as my heart races in anxiety. I hear something quiet, like a whisper, it is another voice. A voice from my present, not my past, telling me to keep on coming, telling me that all will be well. The voice says to keep focused, listen to the knowledge that I have been accumulating and trust the relationship that has been building. I realize this second voice is the correct one to listen to.

Therefore be clear minded and self-controlled so that you can pray. 1 Peter 4: 7b

As I stand here the knowledge I have tells me that yes it is true; the devil is like a lion looking for someone to devour. The devil does it in ways that I just experienced standing on the step stone of knowledge. Those voices of the past rushing through my head showing me scenes that I have forgotten long ago, bringing up memories that are very painful and dark.

I decide to pray, to seek the strength of Jesus. I pray for forgiveness for the sins that have been rushing through my head that I committed. Yes, Jesus took those sins and washed them clean with his blood when I accepted him as my Savior, but I feel the need to give these to Jesus now. I pray to seek the courage, and as I do my faith is increasing, as is my relationship with the Lord. So I go ahead and take that leap to the step stone of self-control. It seemed like a long jump when I was on the step stone of knowledge and when I was in the air, yet when I landed safely and securely I turned to look and I see that the step stone of knowledge seemed to be right next to the stone I now stand on, as do the stones of faith and goodness. I hear a voice tell me that it is okay to use the step stone of knowledge to balance on if I need to, sort of a base to fall back on. So I put my left foot down on the step stone of knowledge and my right foot stays on the step stone of self-control which feels a little wobbly and slippery.

Now the real fight starts. This fight is going to be different, because I will be fighting myself and my sinful nature. I realize that the step stone of goodness was a beginning scene of this fight because I made changes to my outward appearance and actions. I practiced the goodness by being more polite, caring, generous, showing concern, and putting others first. When I practiced that, I still would have thoughts in my head just like the wrong saying people in the Nashville region use. You know the one where they say "Bless your heart!" but in reality they mean "You are so stupid!" Now with this self-control, I have to not just practice or say, I also have to think it, feel it, live it in my heart.

In Matthew chapter 5 there are teachings of Jesus as he sat on a mountainside. These teachings are known as the "Sermon on the Mount". In these teachings he tells us that if you look at another woman lustfully in your heart or mind you have committed adultery with her. In other words Jesus is confirming that our Heavenly Father knows our intentions, our thoughts. He just does not pay attention to what we do on the outside, our actions.

Jesus also tells us that if you say "racca" to someone, or call them a fool you placed yourself in danger of hell. Racca is like saying to someone "Oh you are so stupid", and calling them a fool is a judgment on their character.

I am guilty of both of these examples, looking lustfully and thinking about someone in negative ways; it is a struggle of self. It is at these times I am relying on my own strength and I fail. I will allow the day to day trials get to me, and I fall. I am thankful that my relationship with the Lord is getting stronger each and every day and these times are getting farther and farther apart. I can trust in the Lord to help me in my self-control. It reminds me of these writing's from Paul.

Finally, brothers, whatever is true, whatever is noble, whatever is right, whatever is pure, whatever is lovely, whatever is admirable— if anything is excellent or praiseworthy— think about such things. Whatever you have learned or received or heard from me, or seen in me—put it into practice. And the God of peace will be with you. Philippians 4: 8 – 9

In other words no more stinking thinking!

You were taught, with regard to your former way of life, to put off your old self, which is being corrupted by its deceitful desires; to be made new in the attitude of your minds; Ephesians 4: 22 -23

Do not let any unwholesome talk come out of your mouths, but only what is helpful for building others up according to their needs, that it may benefit those who listen. And do not grieve the Holy Spirit of God, with whom you were sealed for the day of redemption. Get rid of all bitterness, rage and anger, brawling and slander, along with every form of malice. Be kind and compassionate to one another, forgiving each other, just as in Christ God forgave you. Ephesians 4: 29 – 32

I know there is a lot in these verses, but it all has to do with self-control and living the life that God desires of us. These actions are what the world sees and makes their judgments on. I see that I need to cast off my old self, along with the desires that came with that old self. Desires such as thinking bad things about others, or having lustful thoughts in my heart, in other words to continue as I did before. We are called to change, to be the ambassadors of God.

The sins of my past will continue to try and call to me, and the devil will try even harder to devour me with acts of the flesh and the mind. These acts of the flesh include such things as getting impatient, sarcastic, angry, self-centered thoughts of not being worthy, lustful thinking, covetousness and on and on. I must stand firm drawing on my faith and knowledge to bring this goodness to a higher level in my mind and heart. Being good in appearance is not good enough just as the Pharisees did.

He (Jesus) said to them (Pharisees), "You are the ones who justify yourselves in the eyes of men, but God knows your hearts. What is highly valued among men is detestable in God's sight. Luke 16: 15 Parentheses added

This practicing in and of itself is still not enough for me to stand on the step stone of self-control by itself and prepare for the next stone. No, I need to make other changes in my life style. I need to put myself to the side and continue to put others first.

Paul tells us that we are free in Christ.

It is for freedom that Christ has set us free. Stand firm, then, and do not let yourselves be burdened again by a yoke of slavery. Galatians 5: 1

Slavery? Yes! Slavery to what ever it was that held our attention at the bank side before we took that leap to the step stone of faith. Slavery to things like: football, shopping, beauty supplies, cars (racing), television, fishing, partying, gossiping, etc. It was these exact same things that the devil used and will continue to use to make us stumble, try to make us give up and go back to where we came from.

With this freedom comes responsibility. This responsibility is to God of course, but also to others around us, both Christian and non-Christian. To God because we are told that we are the ambassadors for Him to the world. To Christians because they may not have the same understanding that we do and if they see us doing something they may in their minds sin by judging us wrongly. To non-Christians because if they see us doing certain things, it may cause them to see us as Pharisee's and hypocrites; which would give them an excuse to turn away from the hope and freedom that we enjoy. Here are a couple of scripture passages that pretty much sums it all up in this matter.

Everything is permissible"—but not everything is beneficial. "Everything is permissible"—but not everything is constructive. Nobody should seek his own good, but the good of others. I Corinthians 10: 23 – 24

So whether you eat or drink or whatever you do, do it all for the glory of God. Do not cause anyone to stumble, 1 Corinthians 10: 31 – 32a

Here is an example: There are some believers that think it is an absolute sin to partake in any alcoholic drinks. Then there are others who see nothing wrong with having a drink or two. Then there are some who drink to excess all the time. Personally I fall into the middle group; but my thought pattern is this. It is not the fact that I have a few drinks; it is when I do and what I do after them. Let me explain. If I drink and loose my sense of Christianity and act in a way that denies my salvation, then I have sinned. If I drink in front of reformed alcoholics, I take the chance at providing them with a tall temptation, and they may stumble. I must not do anything that would take away from the glory of God. Once I do, I have sinned. Let me tell you now that I have, but then sought the forgiveness of God and received it. There are those however that feel that just one drink is a sin, and that justifies you getting thrown out of their church. I believe that these people are not representing God in a favorable light. After all, that is exactly what the Pharisee's did. Remember the story of the Pharisee and the publican in the synagogue?

To some who were confident of their own righteousness and looked down on everybody else, Jesus told this parable: "Two men went up to the temple to pray, one a Pharisee and the other a tax collector. The Pharisee stood up and prayed about himself: 'God, I thank you that I am not like other men—robbers, evildoers, adulterers—or even like this tax collector. I fast twice a week and give a tenth of all I get.' "But the tax collector stood at a distance. He would not even look up to heaven, but beat his breast and said, 'God, have mercy on me, a sinner.' "I tell you that this man, rather than the other, went home justified before God. For everyone who exalts himself will be humbled, and he who humbles himself will be exalted." Luke 18: 9 – 14

I believe this is a perfect example of why I left the church in the first place. There were far too many judgmental people around. They would speak openly about others and their sins, yet not give one thought to the things that may have been a sin in their own life. If anything in your life takes precedents in your life over matters of God, or if you do things that do not bring glory to God, then you may fall into this category. Seek the Lord and let Him work in your heart, God is just and full of grace, and quick to forgive.

I have come that they may have life, and have it to the full. John 10: 10b

I read this promise from Jesus and I feel like I am ready, feel enabled by the strength of Jesus; I can now stand alone on the step stone of self-control. So I lift my left foot off of knowledge and place it on self-control. It still feels wobbly, but as I stand it gets more stable, sort of like a gymnast on a balance beam. When they get up on it, it takes a second or two for them to gain the balance with their legs a shaking. Let me tell you now, there will be stumbles and times we will fail. Just read this from Paul.

We know that the law is spiritual; but I am unspiritual, sold as a slave to sin. I do not understand what I do. For what I want to do I do not do, but what I hate I do. And if I do what I do not want to do, I agree that the law is good. As it is, it is no longer I myself who do it, but it is sin living in me. I know that nothing good lives in me, that is, in my sinful nature. For I have the desire to do what is good, but I cannot carry it out. For what I do is not the good I want to do; no, the evil I do not want to do—this I keep on doing. Now if I do what I do not want to do, it is no longer I who do it, but it is sin living in me that does it. So I find this law at work: When I want to do good, evil is right there with me. For in my inner being I delight in God's law; but I see another law at work in the members of my body, waging war against the law of my mind and making me a prisoner of the law of sin at work within my members. What a wretched man I am! Who will rescue me from this body of death? Thanks be to God—through Jesus Christ our Lord! Romans 7: 14 – 25a

The key to this somewhat confusing passage is at the very end; my strength to get through this change in my life comes not from myself, but from Jesus Christ my Lord. It is so much easier in this life to follow my sinful desires but that gets me nowhere, and if I am truly committed to a life that leads to rejoicing in the Lord, I must do as Jesus taught and as the apostles taught. Stand strong in the Lord for in this all I am being prepared for the next step.

Other readings for study:

Psalms 16, 2 Corinthians 4: 1 – 6, Mark 9: 42 – 50, 1 Corinthians 10: 13

Chapter 10

Perseverance

Be strong and courageous. Do not be terrified; do not be discouraged, for the LORD your God will be with you wherever you go. Joshua 1: 9b

Here I am standing firm on this step stone feeling like I am getting a handle on self-control when I look down and out to the next step stone which is called perseverance. This stone looks very unstable and my fear starts to creep in slowly at first, then it starts to speed up. Almost the same feelings I had when looking at the step stone I now stand on. This stone is very rounded at the

Step Stones

---

top with a narrow base and it looks like the water rushing around it, if it had just a little more force, could push this stone over into the deepest part of the current. Once again I think that if I jump, and I do mean jump to this stone I can easily loose my balance and fall.

The knowledge that I continue to gain as my faith increases tells me that all will be well. Yet my mind again starts to argue with God and with myself. The devil lion tried very hard to knock me off the step stone of self-control by attacking me in thoughts of self. These came in forms of lies about me, unbelievable pressures from my job, false expectations, and of course attitudes towards others and how I expressed them. I am sure that he will continue to try even harder to make me stumble and fall now that I am thinking of taking the next step of perseverance.

I recall the scripture from Joshua and gain strength in the Lord. I give it all to Him. I pray that it will be okay, no matter what is in store for me. My faith dictates to me now that I must trust in Him, after all, here I am in the middle of the river, I made it this far. If I give up now and turn around, I would be a fool. So I take that jump and land squarely on the step stone of perseverance, pleasantly surprised to find out that I did not fall, that this step stone feels a little more solid than it looks.

My mind races and my heart beats anxiously, waiting for the trials to begin; and they do, the step stone starts to wobble. They start off a little slow like little arguments with my wife and my mind goes to places it should not go. So I pray and ask for forgiveness from the Lord and from my wife. The trials get worse. My relationship with the Lord is increasing though, as does my knowledge and my practicing of goodness and self-control. It does take practice and it is all driven by my faith. I am drawn to this scripture verse.

Consider it pure joy, my brothers, whenever you face trials of many kinds, because you know that the testing of your faith develops perseverance. Perseverance must finish its work so that you may be mature and complete, not lacking anything. James 1: 2 – 3

Pure joy, are you nuts? My selfish instincts tell me this is not going to be good, because the trials are going to come in many different ways. It seems like as I get through one, another one starts, and many are happening at the same time. I think about how real lions hunt their prey. I've seen shows about the great beasts of Africa and how they hunt. They will sit and watch for the weakest of the herd, then slowly stalk them, trying to separate them from the rest of the herd. Then when the timing is right, they give chase and as they are chasing they sometimes swipe at the legs of the antelope or wildebeest or what ever the prey may be. They swipe trying to trip them up so they can pounce and devour. This is the same tactic that the devil uses. He tried it while I was on the step stone of self-control but he aimed at my emotions, my thoughts, my spirituality and my relationship with God. Now he comes for the physical things in my life. This comes in many forms ranging from physical health, financial, relationships with those I come in contact all the time, and even attacking my loved ones in the same manner, all this while still attacking my self-control.

Everything in my nature tells me to run back to the bank I came from because I have seen those of the world prosper, and even when they have trials they don't seem to be like this. Self-control and knowledge tells me to draw on my faith once again and look to God through His word.

After Peter wrote to us about the devil being like a lion, he followed it up with this:

Resist him, standing firm in the faith, because you know that your brothers throughout the world are undergoing the same kind of sufferings. And the God of all grace, who called you to his eternal glory in Christ, after you have suffered a little while, will himself restore you and make you strong, firm and steadfast. To him be the power for ever and ever. Amen. 1 Peter 5: 9 -11

My faith calls out to the knowledge I have gained in my trials. Sometimes it takes a while, but I will search the Holy word of God to see what He has to say about all of this. To my surprise I find that the concept of standing firm is predominant throughout the Bible. Look at these for example:

"Do not be afraid. Stand firm and you will see the deliverance the LORD will bring you today." Exodus 14: 13b

You will not have to fight this battle. Take up your positions; stand firm and see the deliverance the LORD will give you, 2 Chronicles 20: 17a

If you do not stand firm in your faith, you will not stand at all. Isaiah 7: 9b

All men will hate you because of me, but he who stands firm to the end will be saved. Matthew 10: 22

By standing firm you will gain life. Luke 21: 19

Be on your guard; stand firm in the faith; be men of courage; be strong. I Corinthians 16: 13

So then, brothers, stand firm and hold to the teachings we passed on to you, 2 Thessalonians 2: 15a

What do all of these passages have in common? Faith and standing firm in what you know, holding onto what you have learned through experience of others and yourself. We know that what we fight is of another world. Paul tells us this about who are fighting and where they come from.

Put on the full armor of God so that you can take your stand against the devil's schemes. For our struggle is not against flesh and blood, but against the rulers, against the authorities, against the powers of this dark world and against the spiritual forces of evil in the heavenly realms. Ephesians 6: 11 -12

I know far too well, that standing firm and considering it pure joy is extremely hard to do; especially when you are under stress that can be affecting your health and relationships. What I have learned is this: Keep your focus on Jesus and not on yourself or the situation you are in. One only needs to look at the incident of Peter when he tried to walk on the water.

Jesus had fed the five thousand men (not counting women and children), and he sent the disciples out on the Sea of Galilee on a boat while he went to pray. The wind was strong and the disciples were having a hard time trying to row against the wind and the waves. Then Jesus walks out to them on top of the water. The disciples see him, but think he is a ghost, most likely because they are afraid of the raging wind and waves, so they are not thinking straight. They were already tired from distributing food to the multitudes so I imagine they were physically and emotionally drained. Then came the storm and we see this:

But Jesus immediately said to them: "Take courage! It is I. Don't be afraid." "Lord, if it's you," Peter replied, "tell me to come to you on the water." "Come," he said. Then Peter got down out of the boat, walked on the water and came toward Jesus. But when he saw the wind, he was afraid and, beginning to sink, cried out, "Lord, save me!" Immediately

Jesus reached out his hand and caught him. "You of little faith," he said, "why did you doubt?" And when they climbed into the boat, the wind died down. Matthew 14: 27 – 32

Peter gets an adrenaline rush, and thinks that because Jesus is walking on the water, so could he. Peter gets out of the boat and actually starts to walk on the water. However his own fears take over when he takes his eyes off of Jesus sees the waves and the feels the force of the wind. Probably thinking to himself what have I gotten myself into now, and he begins to sink. Peter then looks back to Jesus and cries out, save me and of course Jesus reaches out and catches Peter before he sinks any further. Notice that the wind and waves die down after Jesus came on board with them. This is exactly what happens in our lives; at least I know it does in mine. It goes like this; I am worn out from the trials I am going through. These trials are coming fast from all directions, sometimes in multiples, just like a raging storm. I think I am at my wits end, and then I get a glimpse of Jesus once again. This little glimpse emboldens me, and I think I can do it on my own so I try to overcome whatever it is that I am facing. I look away, just for a moment and the trials and the storms get worse. I start to sink, so I cry out once again to Jesus, and of course he lovingly reaches out his hand to rescue me and the trials and storms calm down.

Now this rescue may not take the trials away or calm the storm down completely, but it does give me the strength and encouragement to endure whatever it may be and yes it is a feeling of joy. I need to keep on seeking Jesus in all circumstances in order to feel the grace of God at all times. Look at what Paul tells us about himself in this passage.

To keep me from becoming conceited because of these surpassingly great revelations, there was given me a thorn in my flesh, a messenger of Satan, to torment me. Three times I pleaded with the Lord to take it away from me. But he said to me, "My grace is sufficient for you, for my power is made perfect in weakness." Therefore I will boast all the more gladly about my weaknesses, so that Christ's power may rest on me. That is why, for Christ's sake, I delight in weaknesses, in insults, in hardships, in persecutions, in difficulties. For when I am weak, then I am strong. 2 Corinthians 12: 7 – 10

In chapter eleven of 2 Corinthians Paul tells of the many physical trials he had gone through. Trials such as being beaten with rods, flogged, stoned to the point of death, being shipwrecked, being in danger in the countryside and in the cities. He had gone without food and exposed to the weather without proper clothing. He spent more times in prison for his beliefs and on and on. Yet, Paul tells us he does not want to talk or brag about what he went through. He could have easily said that I am particularly blessed more than others because God had rescued me from all of these calamities. No, Paul wants to boost about his greatest weakness, the thorn in his flesh. Paul prayed, just like he did in all of his other trials in life for God to take this away. God would not because as Paul tells us; so that he would not become conceited.

So when we cry out to God to save us from what ever our thorn is or storm may be at the time, be sensitive that God may be answering your prayers in a different way than what we would like to have. Stand firm in the faith so that just as with Paul, God's grace will be sufficient for us.

I found that sometimes my prayers are answered in different ways that I would like. Here is an example of this, (my paraphrase). In 2 Kings 5: 1 – 14 we see a story of Naaman and his leprosy. Naaman was a mighty commander in the army of one of Israel's enemies and was inflicted with leprosy. Naaman had an Israelite slave girl who suggested to Naaman's wife that Naaman go see the prophet of God in Israel. Long story short Naaman went and saw Elisha the prophet but Elisha never came out of his house. Elisha just sent a message out to Naaman to go and wash in the Jordan River seven times. Naaman didn't like that answer, so he went away because he thought that there would be some extravagant healing. He wanted to see what Elisha did; you know things like some magic incantation or wand waving. So Naaman went away but his servant went to Naaman and convinced him to do as instructed by Elisha, telling him that if Elisha had told you to do something valiant you would have done it. So why not do as Elsiha said. Naaman changed his mind and went to the Jordan River and washed the seven times. Immediately he was cleansed and healed.

I guess I am like that a lot. I like to things to be grand, and when they are not, I get disappointed. It is at these times the step stone I am standing on gets really unsteady. If I think about it though, that is only my selfishness that is getting in the way of God's plan for me. I have heard people say many times that God is mean because he allowed such and such. Then other people that may have gone through the same type of trial but remain solid Christians rejoice, for the grace they received from that trial.

And we know that in all things God works for the good of those who love him, who have been called according to his purpose. Romans 8: 28

So what direction do you lean? Do you believe that God is unfair, that He did not answer your prayer the way you wanted it to? The step stone will get even more unstable. Or do you believe what Paul tells us? The step stone will become more solid.

For me the step stone has become more solid. Sure the trials are not fun when you are going through them, but if (this is a big if) you keep yours eyes ahead on Jesus and not on the storm; you will make it through stronger than ever. I have also found the trials seem to not last as long either, that they become much easier to cope with. You can actually go through them with joy.

Oh no there is that word again, joy during suffering, trials and storms. Look at this.

Let us fix our eyes on Jesus, the author and perfecter of our faith, who for the joy set before him endured the cross, scorning its shame, and sat down at the right hand of the throne of God. Consider him who endured such opposition from sinful men, so that you will not grow weary and lose heart. Hebrews 12: 2 -3

This resurrection life you received from God is not a timid, grave-tending life. It's adventurously expectant, greeting God with a childlike "What's next, Papa?" God's Spirit touches our spirits and confirms who we really are. We know who he is, and we know who we are: Father and children. And we know we are going to get what's coming to us—an unbelievable inheritance! We go through exactly what Christ goes through. If we go through the hard times with him, then we're certainly going to go through the good times with him! Romans 8: 15 – 17 (The Message)

The New International Version says we are *"heirs of God and co-heirs with Christ"*. Look at what we must do, in Romans 8: 28 we are to love God and He will work out all things to the good for us. All things mean just that, all things. Not just the good that happens in our lives but also the bad/tough times. Then these verses tell us that we are God's children and since Christ went through hard times (sufferings), so shall we. Being called a child of God and co-heirs with

Christ is a joy that I wish everyone could feel. I am, and we are special.

Earlier I mentioned that Paul wrote to the Ephesians that what we do battle with is forces of the spiritual world in the heavenly realms. Peter told us that the devil is like a lion going around trying to devour us. So yes, we do battle the devil, however when I was a child, I heard many people in the church we were attending say that the devil just does not go around and act like he used to. In other words the devil does not inflict us with trials. I guess the devil won those battles with those people. Then again I have been involved with churches that believe that every single thing that goes wrong for them is an attack of the devil. From common colds to losing ones car or house keys to spending too much money, it all becomes an attack of the devil. In a way it is true, it is a result of the original sin when God told Adam that our lives would become hard from dealing with the thorns and thistles of life, to having to work hard all day long to provide our needs. Yes the devil is active and some of his best moves are to get a doubt planted in your head about God and His grace.

Now for some hard teaching that if you understand will make your step stone more solid and prepare you for the next step stone. Paul was left with a thorn in his side for a reason was it not? It was left there In order to keep him from being conceited in his own knowledge and spiritual endurance. So the relationship, knowledge, goodness, and self-control that is ever increasing in our faith leads us to this.

Endure hardship as discipline; God is treating you as sons. For what son is not disciplined by his father? If you are not disciplined (and everyone undergoes discipline), then you are illegitimate children and not true sons.

Moreover, we have all had human fathers who disciplined us and we respected them for it. How much more should we submit to the Father of our spirits and live! Our fathers disciplined us for a little while as they thought best; but God disciplines us for our good, that we may share in his holiness. No discipline seems pleasant at the time, but painful. Later on, however, it produces a harvest of righteousness and peace for those who have been trained by it. Hebrews 12: 7 – 11

I mentioned these verses to some people I knew that thought all bad things were an attack of the devil. They got a blank stare in their eyes, as if they had no way to comprehend this teaching. They looked to God during all trials but never gave a second thought that maybe, just maybe, what they were going through was from God as discipline. In my opinion they gave the devil far too much credit, and when they did not seek God with an open mind and heart to find out what the reason for the trial or storm was, I believe they continued to have hard times because of it.

If you believe what Paul told the Romans about us being children of God and co-heirs with Christ, then you believe we are sons of God. Then the natural process is to believe what we are told here in Hebrews. Yes some trials come from God. Why? The only reason is He loves us, and wants us to progress in the image of Christ. He wants us to stand on solid ground that only He can provide.

When we were living in California we prayed asking that in some way God would open a door to the possibility of us relocating back to the central states region so that we could be closer to our families in Northern Indiana. God answered our prayers. I was transferred to a plant in Nashville, Tennessee which was only a seven hour drive to see our families. With this transfer though came many trials and storms. These trials and storms affected my relationship with my wife, with friends, family and in my professional life. Some of the trials affected me physically, some emotionally, some spiritually. Some were of the devil and some were clear discipline from God. In both cases I learned that for me to survive I had to keep seeking the Lord in all things. Many of my prayers included the question "what would you have me to learn from this?" Many times that question came to mind much later than it should have, and as a result, my trials lasted longer than they should have.

So how can I tell the difference? It sometimes can be confusing. I have found that if the during the trial you take your eyes off of Jesus, or find some seeds of doubt, then it is from the devil. However, if the trial gets you to pray harder and harder, and you find yourself getting drawn closer to God by seeking Him in His word, then that trial is most likely a form of discipline from our Heavenly Father. When this happens, I need to not only ask God, but also myself many questions. Do some deep down soul searching reviewing all the things of my life, and the level of importance they hold in my life. I found that it is okay to ask the Lord to help me stand strong and to help me in my faith. It is okay as long as I am seeking the Lord.

Knowledge led me to this story in Mark. (Paraphrase mine.) A story of a man who brought his demon possessed son to Jesus for healing but Jesus was on top of a high mountain with a few of his disciples. The rest of the disciples were left behind at the base of the mountain. The man asked these disciples to cast out the demon from his son, but they could not and an argument ensued. Jesus came down from the mountain and asked them what they were arguing about.

The man with the possessed son answered that he asked the disciples to drive out the demon, but they could not. (Later Jesus said this type of demon could only be driven out by prayer.) Jesus asked for the man to bring him the boy so he could see him. Then we find this short conversation between the man and Jesus.

When the spirit saw Jesus, it immediately threw the boy into a convulsion. He fell to the ground and rolled around, foaming at the mouth. Jesus asked the boy's father, "How long has he been like this?" "From childhood," he answered. "It has often thrown him into fire or water to kill him. But if you can do anything, take pity on us and help us." "'If you can'?" said Jesus. "Everything is possible for him who believes." Immediately the boy's father exclaimed, "I do believe; help me overcome my unbelief!" Mark 9: 20b – 24

Then Jesus cast out the demon and the boy appeared to be dead but Jesus took care of that also. Do you think that man's faith was increased? Of course it was, and so will ours if and when we get into trials or storms that we find hard to endure. When a trial affects one of our loved ones it is usually harder to think straight and to have the faith that we need. I think this man proves that. So when these trials come I need to remember to just ask God to "help my unbelief". I know when I prayed with a sincere heart my prayers were answered, not always in the way I wanted, but I trust that God knows best.

Other readings for study:
    2 Corinthians 4: 7 – 18, Ephesians 6: 10 – 18, Psalms 22, 2 Corinthians 11

Chapter 11

Godliness

Give thanks to the LORD, for he is good; his love endures forever. Psalm 118: 29

Here I am standing on the step stone of perseverance looking ahead to the next step stone of godliness. I am eager to move on for these last two step stones self-control and perseverance has taken a toll. With the stone of self control came attacks of the mind, emotion, and spiritually. With the stone of perseverance came attacks more of the physical nature, illness, financial, mechanical. It was the physical attacks that became the hardest to endure, yet I found them to be the ones that drew me to a stronger relationship with God. I am more than willing to give my praise to God and thank Him for the strength and ability He has blessed me with, through the presence of His Holy Spirit within me. During these last two steps my faith has increased as did my knowledge of the Lord and my willingness to change from my selfish nature to one that practices goodness by putting others first.

This step stone has started to feel more solid as if I was standing on firmer ground. However, my knowledge that has been ever increasing also tells me to be more wary, not to get over confident in myself or my ability. Paul gives us this warning to be wary. I guess he knew that it becomes easy to stand firm in our own ability out of false ways of thinking. It would only take one temptation to take root and build into a stumbling stone and knock us over.

So, if you think you are standing firm, be careful that you don't fall! No temptation has seized you except what is common to man. And God is faithful; he will not let you be tempted beyond what you can bear. But when you are tempted, he will also provide a way out so that you can stand up under it. 1 Corinthians 10: 12-13

Yes! God is faithful and worthy of me living a godly life. When God provides this way out, we must be aware that He does these sorts of things. We need to be in tune with His spirit and listen to those small voices. It could be in the middle of a storm with waves and winds that want to take us over, or it could come as small temptations that make us look like hypocrites and therefore be a poor ambassador to the world.

I believe I learned this best during a very large storm in my life that affected my physical being. It was October of 2005 and I came home from work early because I felt nauseated and weak. I took a long nap which was out of character for me. Sure I nap like everyone else but my naps usually only last twenty minutes at the most. This nap was about three hours long. I woke up and ate some dinner but immediately felt pressure in my upper left chest. Around five in the afternoon, I asked my wife Sandy to take me to the emergency room because this was not normal.

On our way to the hospital I called our Pastor and told him what was going on, I felt pretty much okay, that I just wanted to make sure. I asked for prayers and of course he said he would make calls to others in the church to start praying.

When we got to the hospital emergency room, they did some quick tests and determined that something was going on in my heart and they would have to do an angioplasty in the morning to see if a stint would take care of this issue. Prior stress tests had revealed that I had a very small blockage in the main artery that feeds blood to the heart itself. The great and awesome news is that God provided a wonderful healing that I never dreamed of, all because of His amazing grace.

My healing is not what taught me about God's faithfulness, and that I was ready for the next step stone. What it did was provide a realization that putting others first is God's way of exhibiting His nature to us. It went down like this.

The emergency room staff and the physicians decided to keep me in the emergency room area for the night because they could monitor my condition better and have better resources in case something worse happened. It was around eleven pm and Sandy had already gone home to get some rest assuring me that she would be back bright and early the next morning to be with me. I was glad she went home to get some rest; I did not want her to get worn out. As I was lying in bed trying to get some rest I started to hear two little boys down the hall screaming and crying. About the same time I heard an older man across the room moaning so load that I thought he would wake the patients on the third floor on the other side of the hospital, if not the dead.

I wanted to get some rest and at this point I was able to allow myself to be afraid of what was going to happen. My selfishness started to grumble and complain within and my mind was going in circles at break neck speeds and it would not stop. My mind went to asking God to make the boys stop crying and the man to stop moaning. I was not really asking but more or less telling God to make them stop. Suddenly out of nowhere I felt a calm of peace come over me and a voice said to try and pray for them. At first I said what? Here I am laying here asking for healing and some rest, what do you mean try praying for them? I heard the voice again, or should I say it was an overwhelming feeling to pray, not for myself but for the boys and the man.

I think I ignored this voice and for some reason decided to ask the emergency room nurse what was going on. She told me that one of the boys who was only four years old and the other one five, appeared to have food poisoning and was having severe intestinal cramps. The old man was in his seventies, and they think he was having a gall bladder attack. By the way I know from experience what a gall bladder attack feels like and the pain is the most severe I have ever had.

The goodness in me responded to the voice urging me to say a prayer for the man that God would relieve him of his pain and allow him to get some rest. I also said a prayer for the little boys that God would heel their cramping and that they too would be able to get some rest. I felt I had to say those same prayers over again and by the third or fourth time I said them, the rooms became quiet. I was able to calm down and get some rest.

The lesson here is that I thought I was standing firm by calling out to God in my need, and by calling our Pastor for prayers. I thought I was standing firm when I felt peace in my faith that God would be with me. Then it happened the crying and the moaning and I was tempted to go self-centered and lose my self-control and start complaining to God about the noise. Then Jesus reached down and grabbed me by the hand and led me to what he would have done; pray for others and put them first. God provided this way out of this temptation to flesh out. Thanks be to God, for He alone is worthy of my praise. God is faithful in all aspects of my life; I just need to stay focused on Jesus.

This provided me with the opportunity and the willingness to take the step to godliness from the step stone of perseverance. This was at the same time an awkward step, even though it felt like the right thing. I knew it was right, yet I was nervous. It had to be the natural progression in the path across the step stones to cross the river.

So what exactly is this step stone of godliness? I looked up the word in the dictionary and it only says, pious. Pious is not what I want; it just sounds like something hypocritical. So I look up the word pious and the second definition is what I thought was the main definition and I would guess the world looks at it this way also. It simply states pretending piety. Isn't the pretending hypocritical? Yes it is if that was the only definition. The first and main definition is godly, devout. This simply means religious or devoted to.

I know I want to be godly and be on this step stone, but I am not sure I want to be known as a godly man because of the way the world sees it; you know the pretending part. I protest, as I have many times during this path of step stones. I don't want to be known as a pious hypocrite, even though I know the true meaning of the word. So I decide to look up the Greek word and the definition. The word is eusebeia which means again simply godliness or piety.

Okay, that didn't do me a whole lot of good. Here I am still at the pretending part. My mind tells me to go back or to stay put. Yes I can be happy, grateful, thankful and ecstatic about being healed; but again this pious part just sounds funny. My relationship with God driven by my faith that has just been increased looks deeper, back to the first definition in the dictionary; godly, devout. My knowledge ever increasing leads me to a Bible dictionary. This tells me the following in part:

"The piety toward God and the proper conduct that springs from a right relationship with Him. It is not belief in itself, but the devotion toward God and love toward man that result from that belief. Religious faith is empty without godliness. It is not right action that is done from a sense of duty, but is the spontaneous virtue that comes from the indwelling Christ and reflects Him." (New

International Bible Dictionary Zondervan Publishing House 1987)

That's it! Of course it is I feel totally comfortable with godliness now. After all God saved my life twice, with the sacrifice of Jesus on the cross, and now with the healing of my heart. Not to mention the valuable lesson learned about imitating Christ by putting others first; even when you are in the middle of a crisis.

The right relationship with God is what I am after; what I want to exhibit. It says it is devotion toward God by showing a love toward man resulting from the belief or faith in God. It is not duty as some people see it, but a spontaneous virtue. In other words it is a natural reaction coming from Christ within us by the presence of the Holy Spirit.

I take that small step to godliness. At first it feels real solid and comfortable but as time wears on this stone starts to rock and shake. I wonder what is going on. I pray, but at times it feels like God has decided to ignore me. The attacks from the self control start to come back at me hard enough that I look down to see if I am still on the step stone of godliness, only to find out that I am, but the water of the river has started to lap at my feet making the stone slippery.

My knowledge that I gained from the previous step stones tells me to be patient. To wait and see what the Lord will do. Maybe this is a test to see what I will do. Will I turn and run? Will I stumble and fall? Will my faith increase?

Just at the right time I came across a Pastor teaching about faith. He states that he has found the perfect statement of faith in his opinion. After hearing it, and reading it over and over, memorizing it, I tend to agree with him.

As for me, I look to the LORD for help. I wait confidently for God to save me, and my God will certainly hear me. Micah 7: 7 (NLT)

Yes the Lord is faithful to us and sometimes he is quiet with us but that is okay. I learn to rely on Him more. Daily I seek Him asking for His strength to make it through the day. I ask for more of Him and less of me; more of His grace, and not my self centeredness. I find the following to be even truer than before.

God, who has called you into fellowship with his Son Jesus Christ our Lord, is faithful. 1 Corinthians 1: 9

We hear a lot in teachings that we need to fear God. Many hear that word fear and take the ugly side of that word. They will say, why should I submit to a God that wants me to fear Him? I must admit that for a long time I also felt that way. After all the first three definitions of the word are these: 1. Anticipation of misfortune or pain, the state of being afraid. 2. Something dreaded. 3. Anxiety. I have now learned that the word fear here is the fourth definition which is; Reverent awe, as of God. I like that and am more than happy to fear God. I can agree now with Solomon when he wrote this proverb.

The fear of the LORD is the beginning of wisdom, and knowledge of the Holy One is understanding. Proverbs 9: 10

Ah there it is. My fears (anxieties) at first caused me to protest this step of godliness. I was anxious and afraid of what I thought was something dreadful. Changing into someone that I was not, changing into someone that I resented as a kid, and for many years after that. The "church people" I knew were so willing to criticize and condemn in the name of the Lord. I just could not possibly be that.

Now because of the great statement of Micah's faith, along with many of those found in the Psalms, my knowledge is starting to turn into understanding. I am seeing things with a different view now; a view from the opposite side of the cross. When I was first starting on this path across the river I was approaching the cross from the front looking at Jesus paying my price. Now after my big leap to faith, the change in me to reflect goodness, the knowledge I gained, and the strength given to me during my battles of self-control and my learning to persevere, I find myself on the back side of the cross seeing the world as Jesus sees it. People that are hurting and seeking; being afraid the same as I was. Thinking we are going to lose our independence when the exact opposite is true. As I went through all of these steps, each with their own degree of difficulty, God lead me in a gentle way. In doing so our relationship grew to a point where I now feel God's presence in all situations. If I do not feel His presence, it is because of my own doing. The change in my life is done freely; it is not forced upon me.

Oh do not get me wrong here, I am a sinner and find myself seeking the grace and mercy of God for not representing Him in a positive manner. The freedom I have is also a two edged sword that both allows me to exercise my personality, and allows me the opportunity to get caught up in the world and flesh out.

I am not alone in this. Just take one look at one of the godliest men that ever lived: King David of Israel. God proclaims him to be a man after his own heart.

He testified concerning him: 'I have found David son of Jesse a man after my own heart;

he will do everything I want him to do.' Acts 13: 22b

Yet David had his faults. He had the husband of the woman that he had an affair with murdered, when he found out that she became pregnant. David did this because he could not get the husband to be with her, which would have covered up his (David) sin. He went into the temple and ate of the consecrated bread reserved for the high priests when he was hungry and defiled the temple. Yet he wrote wonderful Psalms of praise and worship to God almighty and he was forgiven and given a place of honor as being the one whom Jesus Christ the Son of God would descend from.

In the effort to be godly, I find that it is still a struggle of self-control and perseverance, only in a different way. I look again to David and his Psalms to see that I am not alone; I am just being a fallible human man and find myself at odds with individuals that just make me angry. I do not want to be angry; I feel that it does not represent God to the world very well. So I struggle, get confused, and if I am not careful, can be devoured by the old lion the devil. Looking to the Bible once again I find this from David:

In your anger do not sin; when you are on your beds, search your hearts and be silent. Psalms 4: 4

David in his godliness repented of his sins immediately when he became aware of them and he also brought his feelings of anger and frustrations to God. You see David wrote some Psalms of vengeance; some of which are shocking if you read them casually and not look into what he was doing. Take for instance this excerpt from Psalms 109.

O God, whom I praise, do not remain silent, for wicked and deceitful men have opened their mouths against me; they have spoken against me with lying tongues. With words of hatred they surround me; they attack me without cause. In return for my friendship they accuse me, but I am a man of prayer. They repay me evil for good, and hatred for my friendship. Psalms 109: 1 – 5

Exactly how I feel at times. David even goes on to pray for things I would never dream of. Although, I must admit at times I have thought some hateful things about people. David goes on with this.

May his days be few; may another take his place of leadership. May his children be fatherless and his wife a widow. May his children be wandering beggars; may they be driven from their ruined homes. May a creditor seize all he has; may strangers plunder the fruits of his labor. May no one extend kindness to him or take pity on his fatherless children. Psalms 109: 8 - 12

Step Stones

Here David is asking for God to destroy a man, leave his wife a widow, his children fatherless, and then for his children to be outcasts. Man that just sits really bad with me, for I know what it is to have a widow for a mother, and in some ways to be treated as outcasts from the church. But David is doing the only thing a godly person can do; that is to bring it to God. After all if we are developing a strong relationship with God, would we not bring everything to Him in conversation just as we would if we are talking to a friend? I believe that God would rather have us bring it to Him than to one of our close friends. After all a friend might not take that kind of talk in the proper manner. If we cannot vent to God our Father, who can we vent to? That is the ultimate sign in my opinion of living a Godly life. Bringing our problems to Him and not release it on the world.

When I have come to understand that, I look ahead to see what the next step stone may bring. It keeps getting better all the time, and my trust and dependence on the Lord grows deeper. I can agree with the prophet of old when he stated this:

"the righteous will live by his faith" Habakkuk 2: 4b

My faith has been increased from seeing the goodness in myself that comes from Jesus Christ, from the knowledge I have gained and continue to gain, from learning the truth of self-control and from persevering in the faith that no matter what happens in this life, I can count on God being there for me, even at the times I feel He is silent.

I am now more alive than I have ever felt before. I find myself praying more often than I did before. Not formal prayers but quick ones of praise, thanksgiving and many times a cry for help. Learning from my trials and blessings, I find this passage, and for the first time, I can understand it.

Be joyful always; pray continually; give thanks in all circumstances, for this is God's will for you in Christ Jesus. 1 Thessalonians 5: 16 - 18

My joy is such that I am in reverence and awe of the Mighty God and am looking forward to the next step stone. Before I take that step, let me leave you with this verse that can help you in all situations. Our kingdom that we belong to in Christ will not falter, it will not fail.

Therefore, since we are receiving a kingdom that cannot be shaken, let us be thankful, and so worship God acceptably with reverence and awe, Hebrews 12: 28

Other readings for study:

Psalms 42, 48, 51, 118, Ephesians 4: 17 – 32, 1 Timothy 6: 6

Chapter 12

Brotherly Kindness

Be devoted to one another in brotherly love. Honor one another above yourselves. Romans 12: 10

And he has given us this command: Whoever loves God must also love his brother. 1 John 4: 21

Standing on the step stone of godliness, I look ahead and take the next step. It is just a short step and the stone looks solid and firm. I take that step with confidence only to find out the appearance is really deceiving. Just as I thought that godliness would be an easier step stone because of the trials endured while on self-control and perseverance, only to find out that in fact it was a very difficult stone to balance on. It was harder to keep the balance because of the fact that even though I went through the self-control and perseverance with the devil lion swiping at my legs, I found out that at this step, the attacks did not stop. They came in more subtle ways and I had to be on my guard all the time. That is where the praying continually came in and had to be consciously practiced. Thank God for His Holy Spirit to encourage me, and to bring to remembrance this truth.

I can do everything through him who gives me strength. Philippians 4: 13

It's almost comical at times that in my toughest moments this verse would pop up in my head along with a few other verses concerning faith. Now as I am standing on this step stone called brotherly kindness, I am struggling to keep my balance. The stone that looked solid in fact was sitting in some loose gravel, and we all know what happens to loose gravel in a current of rushing river water.

At first I feel uncomfortable on this step stone. It is not my nature to go out of the way to be kind, besides I was thinking that this would be a repeat of the step stone of goodness. Oh how wrong I could be. Even with the knowledge I have gained I really was unprepared for this step stone. Goodness has to do with an attitude change towards people in general. Goodness was the step prior to the step of self-control and it was still easy to not show the goodness, to get in the flesh and be worldly.

Then I thought that this step would be to show extra goodness (kindness) to the brothers and sisters in Christ, you know fellow believers. This is of course true but as I found out this really is much more, much deeper than that. Let me explain.

When I look up the Greek translation for brotherly kindness it gives me the word "philadelphia", and this means brotherly love. Okay, you say how does that make it deeper? It all comes down now to the question of who is a brother (or sister) that qualifies this extra step called brotherly kindness. The answer can be found in Paul's letter to the Colossians.

And you have been given fullness in Christ, who is the head over every power and authority. Having been buried with him in baptism and raised with him through your faith in the power of God, who raised him from the dead. Colossians 2: 9 & 12

When you were dead in your sins and in the uncircumcision of your sinful nature, God made you alive with Christ. He forgave us all our sins, having cancelled the written code, with its regulations that was against us and that stood opposed to us; he took it away, nailing it to the cross. Colossians 2: 13 – 14

Any man, woman or child that has given themselves to Christ and confessed that Jesus is the holy Son of God and that his death upon the cross paid for their sins is a brother or sister in Christ and worthy of brotherly kindness. I can admit that this is not always easy because many in the church can be arrogant, snobbish, selfish, and may have many interests that just do not agree with my personality. In this category you can find many people that act very pious and I am going to one of the negative definitions here. You know the ones that act or pretend piety, a false or pretentious outward attitude. You may also find the Pharisee's in this group. The ones that act as if they have the truth and you do not just because you may worship in a different way than they do. The list here can go on and on but you can see that even though others are different than me that does not make them any less of a Christian than I am. I am not capable of seeing their hearts, their thoughts, only God can do that, so I must as a child of God; assume that they are truly Christian. I must express brotherly kindness to them.

So what exactly is this brotherly kindness and how is it different from goodness? Again we can find the answer from Paul and his letter to the Galatians.

Carry each other's burdens and in this way you will fulfill the law of Christ. If anyone thinks he is something when he is nothing he deceives himself. Each one should test his own actions. Then he can take pride in himself, without comparing himself to somebody else, Galatians 6: 2 – 4

Let us not become weary in doing good, for at the proper time we will reap a harvest if we do not give up. Therefore as we have opportunity, let us do good to all people, especially to those who belong to the family of believers. Galatians 6: 9 – 10

    I am led to the opinion that it is my responsibility to give others the benefit of the doubt. By this I mean to humble myself by putting others first, just as Christ instructed us to do. I have no reason to judge others intentions, otherwise I end up thinking that I am something when I am not. Once I start to judge or label others, I end up being mixed into the false pride category. It is when I can look at others, treat them with the kindness and goodness in a manner that I would like to be treated, and with no inner thoughts of a judgmental attitude then and only then can I take that pride in myself for not comparing.

    I know we all make judgments at one time or another. Yet a judgment can be both good and bad. It is what I do with it in my mind or maybe verbally. Let's say I do not like the color red. I make the judgment to not paint my living room red. That is a judgment that does no harm. Now let's say my friends go out and paint their living room red. I go over to their house, see the living room painted red and tell them that I hate it; it just does not look good. That is abuse of judgment that only stands to hurt my friends. So I have to learn that even if I do not like something, I must try to accept it and be happy for them.

Okay, that was a lame example of good and bad judgment. Let's put it this way: If a judgment does no harm then it is good. If the judgment does harm or hurts someone then it is bad. Let's remember that even if you do not express the judgment and keep it to yourself it can still be a harmful judgment. Remember the teaching of Jesus about looking at another person lustfully causes you to commit adultery with them in your heart. Well I would say a judgment in the heart or mind causes you to be un-Christian like and guilty of thinking yourself better than others.

I am beginning to understand this concept of brotherly kindness a little better. It is still a shaky stone and I wonder why. I give it some thought and it goes back to my sinful nature of the flesh. Back to the way I treated others prior to my accepting Christ. As a human I am weak and like to puff myself up, sometimes in ways that tear others down, even the ones I love. I am feeling good about God's myriad of blessings in my life, and my nature wants to think that God is blessing me because I am doing good. Then I come across this again and find out that no matter what I do, I can not save myself or make my standing any better.

For it is by grace you have been saved, through faith—and this not from yourselves, it is the gift of God— not by works, so that no one can boast. For we are God's workmanship, created in Christ Jesus to do good works, which God prepared in advance for us to do. Ephesians 2: 8 - 10

A subtle yet effective reminder that God, through His grace saved me and it was a gift. I can do nothing to add to it and therefore have no reason to boast. It reminds me that we (brothers and sisters in Christ) not me are God's workmanship and we are created to behave in ways that glorify God, through our good works of kindness, humility, and by putting other's first. This is how God planned it out for us. This is how the good news of Jesus Christ has spread throughout the world. It comes down to being unified in our message. If you look at other religions you see a lot of emphasis on the self and what individuals can get. I fear that is happening today as I mentioned earlier in the Love Your Neighbor chapter. Much of today's preaching consists of the benefits (prosperity) you will get from God. So I fear that much of the church today is losing credibility with the world. With Christianity it is supposed to be all about other's, because God thought about us when He did not have to. God's desire to have a relationship with His creation is the reason He did what He did.

I look down and see that the step stone of godliness seems to have moved closer to the stone of brotherly kindness almost as if it was trying to become one large solid stone instead of two. What made this happen? I think that as I gain knowledge, and my relationship with God is strengthened, I begin to understand that God's message from the beginning till now how has never changed. God desires for us to be unified as Christians. The differing denominations are okay as long as one denomination does not think itself better than another. As long as the message of God's love and grace expressed through Jesus Christ, and that we all have the Holy Spirit alive in us is taught. The way we worship is up to each individual style.

Why is this unity so important? Jesus himself prayed that we would be unified.

My prayer is not for them alone. I pray also for those who will believe in me through their message, that all of them may be one, Father, just as you are in me and I am in you. May they also be in us so that the world may believe that you have sent me. I have given them the glory that you gave me, that they may be one as we are one: I in them and you in me. May they be brought to complete unity to let the world know that you sent me and have loved them even as you have loved me. John 17: 20 - 23

If Jesus prayed this prayer for future believers (us), then it must be important. The churches today must understand this or they corrupt the message that Jesus wanted us to bring to the world. (See the great commission Matthew 28 16 – 20 & Acts 1: 7 – 8.) We must as a unified church express grace and peace to each other (brotherly kindness); so that the world can see it and know that Jesus was sent here by God. After all Jesus lives in us through his Holy Spirit and God the Father lives in Jesus, then does this not mean that God is in us? Of course it does.

I guess like the previous step stones on this path across the rampaging river of life, this brotherly kindness will take a daily effort, a conscious decision to walk in a way that honors God. Yet because of my flesh and my selfishness this step stone has caused me more struggles than I anticipated. I know that I need to work on this because it will strengthen my relationship with God. After all, how could my life be a testimony if I learn and practice all of these steps yet ignore this one? So I pray and look to God and His word seeking some guidance. I find it in one of Paul's letters.

I urge you to live a life worthy of the calling you have received. Be completely humble and gentle; be patient, bearing with one another in love. Make every effort to keep the unity of the Spirit through the bond of peace. There is one body and one Spirit—just as you were called to one hope when you were called— one Lord, one faith, one baptism; one God and Father of all, who is over all and through all and in all. Ephesians 4: 1b - 6

This urging of Paul's is more than a recommendation, it is almost a command. To live a life worthy of the calling from God would be to live a godly life. When I was on the step stone of goodness, I learned that we as Christians are ambassadors of God to the world. (2 Corinthians 5: 20) We do this not by our strength or effort but by the Holy Spirit living within us. We allow the Holy Spirit to show us how to live as Jesus did. After all

Jesus humbled himself to our level. Jesus could have come and made himself King over all creation in a giant earthly palace and it still would have been a humbling experience for him compared to his heavenly kingdom. Jesus was gentle in everything he did. Look at how he dealt with the common man, the ill, the poor and the "sinners". He definitely was patient in all that he did. One just needs to look at his time with the disciples and see how he handled their bickering over who would be the greatest. Then of course, Jesus puts up with us (bear with) in love. We are not worthy of God's grace, yet it is expressed daily or should I say constantly to us.

When we consciously seek and practice this nature of Jesus, we as the body of Christ (the Church) can show the world unity in the message. How great of a witness we can be to the rest of the world. Even David knew the blessings of unity in God. Just look at what he wrote here.

How good and pleasant it is when brothers live together in unity! For there the Lord bestows his blessing, even life forevermore. Psalm 133: 1 & 3b

With the unity comes the blessing of God. He will show His favor with us when we practice his grace and love. After all, because He has showed it to us, we need to follow His will.

He has showed you, O man, what is good. And what does the Lord require of you? To act justly and to love mercy and to walk humbly with your God. Micah 6: 8

I like many people misunderstood what "to humble yourself" really means. I thought that it meant to be meek and wimpy, to let others walk over you. It does not. When people act that way it gives the impression that we are weak and need a "crutch" to get us through life. When in fact to be humble is to know ourselves and not think to highly of ourselves. God created each of us with a distinct personality and we need to use that personality in a godly manner. God prepared us in advance to treat others as someone worthy of love and kindness, just as God showed us in His love for us.

Jesus told us in Mathew 5 that we are the salt and light of the world. My contention is that when we try to act in ways contrary to our personalities then we are salt that has lost its saltiness. When we think to highly of our self then we are covering the light that God gave us.

My wife has worked in public places and at times is required to work on Sunday. She has noticed along with her co-workers, that people who come into the restaurant that she works at on Sunday's, are generally meaner, grumpier than people who come other days of the week. She says that you can tell they just came from church by the way they dress. You know the kids are all in little suits and dresses, mom and dad are dressed in their "Sunday Best". After she mentioned this to me I started to notice the personalities of these people. I can attest they are shorter with other people, they are rude and impolite, and have a general attitude that others around them are beneath them. Here is the disclaimer; not all are this way. There are many who get it and understand, but there are a lot that fall into the previous category. When this happens where is the saltiness? Where is their light? It is at these times that the world sees these actions, even if it is only a few, and looks negatively at all Christians.

Step Stones

In the earlier chapter about Christians I pointed out that seventy-six percent of Americans say they are Christian. Yet in other recent polls it shows that less than half will attend church on a semi-regular basis. I wonder why this is. Is it because they will see the hypocrisy in the church? When we go out into the public as Christians, we are Christians every minute of every day, and the way we act is our testimony.

This step stone is feeling firmer now, I look down now to see that the stone of godliness is touching the stone of brotherly kindness, and the next stone which is love is only a few inches away. This next step stone is actually resting on the bank leading to the path that I was trying to get to.

Yet; I stand here wondering why these stones have moved so close to each other and that it took me so long to notice. Then it comes to me, all three of these stones are important, and must be practiced as a Christian every moment of every day. Not in my strength, but the strength of the Holy Spirit within me. Drawing on my knowledge and goodness bonded in faith, I am reminded of this:

Now faith is being sure of what we hope for and certain of what we do not see. Hebrews 11: 1

And now these three remain: faith, hope and love. But the greatest of these is love. 1 Corinthians 13: 13

It is at this point it all comes together in my mind. This is all a relationship with God the Father through Jesus Christ my Savior. It started with faith, but that is not the end. As I was standing on every step stone across this river, I had to draw on my faith and my relationship with God. When I did this through prayer and worship, my hope was always confirmed. Godliness was a direct result of seeing and feeling God involved in every aspect of my life, taking me through the rough times, helping me change or conform to His will. Brotherly Kindness was the next result that sprung up in my hope which is a sure thing. Being kind to all men, women and children is a way of honoring God, because He did so for me. Faith, hope, and love are all about the relationship. The greatest being love, because that is what God is.

And so we know and rely on the love God has for us. God is love. Whoever lives in love lives in God, and God in him. In this way, love is made complete among us so that we will have confidence on the day of judgment, because in this world we are like him. 1 John 4: 16 - 17

Other readings for study:

    Matthew 7: 1 – 5, 1 Corinthians 12: 12 – 27, 2 Corinthians 5: 16 – 20,

Chapter 13

Love a Solid Rock Bridge

This is love: not that we loved God, but that he loved us and sent his Son as an atoning sacrifice for our sins. Dear friends, since God so loved us, we also ought to love one another. No one has ever seen God; but if we love one another, God lives in us and his love is made complete in us. 1 John 4: 10 - 12

Looking down at this last step stone I see that it is resting on a slippery muddy spot of the bank. This puzzles me at first then I notice that the step stones of godliness and brotherly kindness have lined up in way that almost resembles a brace for the stone

Step Stones

called love. I am puzzled even more. Then I begin to understand. This last step is not going to be an easy one. Taking a better look at the way the stone is resting, I can see that it is ready to slide on the mud into the river. If I step on the stone incorrectly the stone may teeter and slide. Should I step onto the front, middle or the far end? My mind and heart are racing with thoughts of pain that has been associated with love in my past. What if I fail at this, as I did before when I tried to love, and be loved? Before I step, I stop and think about what this will require of me. My answer comes quickly when I give this thought process to the Lord in prayer. Just as I have relied on my faith in the Lord for all of the other steps, I must also rely on Jesus in this one.

Before I step I pause again, trying to understand a little better. How I wish I can be like some people that just accept and go with it, not thinking twice. I on the other hand was created to be a little quizzical. You know the one that wants to understand the why's, how's and what for's. Once I get it, it is easy for me to apply that to other things. With this love thingy, I am more hesitant than I probably should be. So I stand on this step stone of brotherly kindness wondering.

The concept of love to a man such as myself, or should I say as a mere human is not one that is acceptable. Sure I love my wife, family, home, job, car, and church; but is this the love that is meant by this last step stone? I do not think it is. I believe that some of the things I said I love may only be a strong fondness or caring for; you could say I like very much. I know I love my wife and would do anything for her, but for the other things I mentioned, I just do not know.

The English language actually distorts what love is and then our society of me first has distorted it even more. Maybe polluted it is the better concept. Take the Greek language, there are five distinct words that describe what we lump into one word; love. These five words are:

Thelema – Desire or as we would say "I would love to have this or that". In our society we use this meaning far too much and this in my opinion distorts the word, to the point that the word almost becomes meaningless.

Storge – Affection or a love within the family. A parent will have a feeling of love for a child no matter what that child has done or how they turn out when they are adults. The parents will love that child, even though they are disgusted with them and want nothing to do with them. Our prisons are loaded with people that have parents and family members that hate what they did, but love them anyway.

Philia - This is where the brotherly kindness comes in. Covered in the previous chapter and I would dare to guess, is the least used meaning of love in our society. O sure, we may act like and practice on the outside, but what really goes on inside is the answer.

Eros – Passionate, sensual, desire or romantic love. Our society has used this to pollute the word love more than anything else. When in fact our society has driven lust into the definition and that really has no place in this conversation.

Agape – This is true love. A love a man or woman has for their spouse. This love is one that God has for all mankind, regardless of who or what we are. This love, when you look at the divorce rates in our society, is probably not practiced very much. The best definition for agape love will be discussed a little later on.

Knowing what these definitions are, I can understand where my hesitation comes from. Our society along with my selfish human nature makes it hard to practice any of these consistently. When it is not consistent; then is it love, goodness, brotherly kindness, or something else? From my experience I can also say with honesty that you do not see much of this practiced in the church very much either.

You see my hesitation comes from my past. My father died suddenly when I was only ten years old. I am okay with that, or should I say I should have been okay with that. It is all the other garbage that went on after dad's death that eventually drove me away from the church, and from God. My mother was strong in her faith and it was her prayer life that kept her going. She had faith first and foremost in God and His grace. She then had faith in family, that they would be there to help her, then faith in her church who also was supposed to help. After all it is a sign of true religion to take care of widows is it not?

Religion that God our Father accepts as pure and faultless is this: to look after orphans and widows in their distress and to keep oneself from being polluted by the world. James 1:27

My mother kept her end of it; she did not allow herself to become polluted by the world or by her selfish human nature which we are all born with. The church did not hold up their end, neither did members of our family on my father's side. Before I go on any further, I want you all to know that God has helped me to see and understand that we all fail in many areas and I have forgiven. I failed in my own rebellious ways which led to a prodigal life. It is only by the grace of God given to us in abundance that I made it. I fail, but keep on persevering in Jesus' strength, not my own. I believe that my mother's prayers for me and just seeing the example she set in how she handled herself in grace though trials is what brought me back to God.

Shortly after my dads death I recall that the church pounced on her trying to accuse her of not giving enough money to the church, in other words holding out. She was ostracized for not having good enough clothes, and for all things allowing her boys to have long hair and to listen to rock music. All of this as she struggled to put us kids through an expensive Christian school education. The list could go on, but I will hold it to just those few things without anymore details. In my mind, if the church was holding up their end of what James described as true and pure, they would have been there to help with our education, with clothing, with grace and support.

Also after my dads death we as a family were pretty much shut out by family on dad's side. My grandfather would not let us come over any more, so our aunts and uncles kind of took their queue from him. They did not hold up to their part of what James described as true and pure. I have four grandchildren of my own now, and I can tell you that if anything ever happened to my son or daughter in-law, I would do everything possible to make sure my grandkids had the means, love and encouragement they needed to get by in this world. Enough said on that also. Stirring up old wounds serve no purpose. I can thank God for his healing grace in my emotions, for loving me and leading me through this path. I also thank God for helping me see that I handled many of these hurts, pains, and disappointments in ways that hurt me. I am not trying to blame anyone for my leaving God and the church. What I did, I did, no one else but me. I own up to my mistakes and have sought the forgiveness through Jesus crucified, and have received it.

Okay, I'm ready for that step, I now realize that it does not matter what part of the stone I step on, I am not going to do it in my strength, but in the grace of God. Since we saw at the end of the last chapter that God is love, there must also be a description of God that will help us to understand.

And he passed in front of Moses, proclaiming, "The LORD, the LORD, the compassionate and gracious God, slow to anger, abounding in love and faithfulness, maintaining love to thousands, and forgiving wickedness, rebellion and sin. Exodus 34: 6 -7b

The LORD is compassionate and gracious, slow to anger, abounding in love. He will not always accuse, nor will he harbor his anger forever; he does not treat us as our sins deserve or repay us according to our iniquities. Psalm 103: 8 - 10

I look at these two scripture passages, seeing that God is exactly as how we want to be treated. We fight and bicker in this world because we think the world is not fair to us. We desire for love, but end up looking for it in the wrong frame of mind. We look with our interests in mind, not others. We look through selfish stained vision. I can say this because I was what I just described. I wanted love and to be loved so badly that I did not realize I was loved, not just by God but by others around me. In my twisted worldly thought process that was fueled by the father of lies the devil himself, I thought that God took away my father, family, church, and made life miserable for my mother because He was a mean God. I thought I did something wrong. Then later on in life when my first marriage failed (most of it my fault), I once again felt like love was being yanked away from me. In essence, I spent about twenty of my years running, looking for love, never finding it, so I kept searching. The whole time if I would have stopped to listen in the quiet, I would have been able to hear the peace found only in the grace of God.

I have made my share of mistakes in this life and many I am ashamed of. I have found true peace through repentance and learning to accept love from God and from those around me. It started when I was at my worst. I know that if it was not for my wife and the love she showed me (even though it was hard for her); I probably would still be running. Sure I started back into the church before her, but it was her grasp of love as expressed through compassion, patience, faithfulness, and allowing God's grace to work in her, that I was able to see true love for the first time. Let's not forget I am talking about agape love, not the other definitions that we distort love with.

So if God is love and I can see what God's character is in the two scriptures from Exodus and Psalms, how can I apply God's character to me? Jesus explained it best when he spoke of putting others first and to love our neighbor as ourselves. Yet, this is still hard because my nature is one of selfishness. Well, that is what this step stone path was all about; a path that taught me to live a life that truly honors God above all else. Paul wrote this to the Ephesians.

Be imitators of God, therefore, as dearly loved children and live a life of love, just as Christ loved us and gave himself up for us as a fragrant offering and sacrifice to God. .. Submit to one another out of reverence for Christ. Ephesians 5: 1 – 2 & 21

Imitators of God! Live a life of love! Give of yourself and submit to one another to show honor to Christ! Hard words to live by and impossible if Christ is not in my life. I think I often held back because of that word submit. It implies losing our personality, but actually it emboldens me.

Here is a scripture passage telling us exactly what love is. I think this passage is used so much I believe it has lost its significance. What I mean is, we look at it and think it is corny because we see this on posters, often not giving any credit to the scripture passage. It is used at weddings for Christians and for non-Christians. We use it because it sounds so nice and makes us say; "That is nice". When in fact, it is a perfect description of God, and if we are to imitate God we must practice this every day.

Love is patient, love is kind. It does not envy, it does not boast, it is not proud. It is not rude,

it is not self-seeking, it is not easily angered, it keeps no record of wrongs. Love does not delight in evil but rejoices with the truth. It always protects, always trusts, always hopes, always perseveres. Love never fails.
1 Corinthians 13: 4 – 8a

- Love is patient – slow to anger.
- Love is kind – compassionate.
- Does not envy – gracious.
- Does not boast – gracious.
- It is not proud – gracious.
- Not rude – compassionate.
- Not self-seeking – abounding in love.
- Not easily angered – slow to anger.
- Keeps no record of wrongs – gracious and slow to anger.
- Does not delight in evil – faithfulness and gracious.
- Rejoices in the truth – faithfulness.
- Always protects – faithfulness and abounding in love.

- Always trusts – gracious and faithfulness.
- Always hopes – compassionate and abounding in love.
- Always perseveres – faithfulness.
- Love never fails – Always, God is Love.

Keep in mind here, that this last step stone is the one that anchors all the other steps. This stone is the reason for the other steps, and if you do not get to this one, all the other steps become a clanging in the wind. Paul put a disclaimer in just before he wrote the above description of love.

If I speak in the tongues of men and of angels, but have not love, I am only a resounding gong or a clanging cymbal. If I have the gift of prophecy and can fathom all mysteries and all knowledge, and if I have a faith that can move mountains, but have not love, I am nothing. If I give all I possess to the poor and surrender my body to the flames, but have not love, I gain nothing. 1 Corinthians 13: 1 - 3

In other words, I can have the faith, the goodness, the knowledge, practice self-control, persevere through trials, be godly and express brotherly kindness but do not step onto this stone of love and practice it, what do you have? (Many non-Christians have these same characteristics). Or where are you in life, in your walk with Jesus? Just standing in the river with life flowing past you and stuck with feelings that overwhelm.

How can I really know when I have taken this last step? My guess is when I can say in all honesty that nothing comes before my relationship with God through Jesus. Be an imitator of God, to show honor and glory to God and to Jesus.

Whoever claims to live in him must walk as Jesus did. 1 John 2: 6

Now I am back to faith, because it takes faith to truly walk as Jesus did. Putting others first, looking with compassion on the sick, the homeless, the dirty and smelly of this world. Do not treat anyone better than anyone else. The list goes on and on. Just read the gospels and study Jesus, his words, his actions, see this and see that the Lord is good.

Do not love the world or anything in the world. If anyone loves the world, the love of the Father is not in him. For everything in the world—the cravings of sinful man, the lust of his eyes and the boasting of what he has and does—comes not from the Father but from the world. The world and its desires pass away, but the man who does the will of God lives forever. 1 John 2: 15 -17

With God we will gain the victory, and he will trample down our enemies. Psalms 60: 12

Here I am still standing with one foot on the step stone of brotherly kindness with the other raised ready to step onto the last stone of love, fearful that this love thing will hurt. I start to cry within my self and my cry goes out to God seeking Him and His grace through Jesus.

Hear my cry, O God; listen to my prayer. From the ends of the earth I call to you, I call as my heart grows faint; lead me to the rock that is higher than I. Psalms 61: 1 – 2

I cried! That seems weird to me, you see I just don't cry. I tend to hold it in and keep my emotions to myself. After my dad's death, I was scolded for crying by an uncle. He told me that I could not cry in front of my mother, she needed me to be strong. So I didn't and now I know in hindsight that my uncle did not just take away my emotional and spiritual development. He also took away the opportunity for my mother to be a mother to me. After all that is what family is for; to share in our joys and our hurts. That is how we grow and learn.

Sure I have cried maybe a half dozen times in thirty plus years since, but they almost always were fueled by alcohol. But now I find myself tearing up at stories that come out of this world. Stories of children being hurt by their parents, elderly folks being hurt by their children, stories of homelessness, and of great pain in this most advanced society that man has ever known. This world just does not make sense to me anymore. Terrible times indeed!

I even find myself getting emotional while watching movies. What am I nuts? At first I thought it was because I was just getting older, but I was wrong. The truth of the matter is this. While I was standing with one foot poised to take that step I did not realize that the stone of love kind of slid into place right under my foot, I had one foot resting on it with out even giving it any thought.

What does this crying about others pain have to do with love? I really do not know; but I do know this, it is a sign that my heart has been softened. I found out that we are to be imitators of Jesus and I find this story of Jesus and his love and how he expressed it. It is the story of Lazarus who had died four days earlier.

When Jesus saw her weeping, and the Jews who had come along with her also weeping, he was deeply moved in spirit and troubled... Jesus wept. Then the Jews said, "See how he loved him!" John 11: 33, 35 – 36

The Jews in this situation looked at Jesus weeping and said the same thing we do today. "He is crying because he loved the one that died." I believe that is true but I look at verse 33 of this scripture and see a bigger reason for Jesus to weep. Jesus saw the ones that were close to Lazarus and they were hurting, so he was deeply moved and troubled in his spirit. It was an expression of love, not just for Lazarus but for his family and friends.

David knew this when he cried out in Psalms 61, that it would not be his effort to achieve this step. No it would be God who is the rock that is higher than any of us. God would achieve this love in us through His Holy Spirit dwelling in us and working in us. David followed the above with this.

Find rest, O my soul, in God alone; my hope comes from him. He alone is my rock and my salvation; he is my fortress, I will not be shaken. My salvation and my honor depend on God; he is my mighty rock, my refuge. Trust in him at all times, O people; pour out your hearts to him, for God is our refuge. Psalms 62: 5 - 8

Yes my rest is in God completely. Now I find myself when I cry saying a prayer to God immediately, and the Lord tells me, yes I have it. I have the love that is a love that truly cares for others, a love that hurts when others hurt. One that is compassionate, forgiving, shows kindness and goodness to all mankind not a select few. Sure I get upset at people for what they do to me and to others; but I am learning to lift the situation up in prayer and give it to God. My perfection is not complete and it will only be complete when I am taken to share in the glories of heaven with Jesus my Savior.

I am also finding this at work which is in agreement with what David wrote. My hope comes from God alone, my salvation and honor depend on God. So I guess it just follows that the love I now have for others is really not my own, but it is God's love working through me. Sure I have to take that step onto the stone but as soon as I tried to do it, it was God who carried it out.

We tell ourselves in this society not to care, that it is weak to show compassion and love. These types of thoughts are the enemies that pursue us, and are the very reason this society is heading downhill very quickly. Only God and his love and grace can overcome, and we are to be the instruments of that grace. Only Christ can work this out through us as Christians, the Church his body.

I have been crucified with Christ and I no longer live, but Christ lives in me. The life I live in the body, I live by faith in the Son of God, who loved me and gave himself for me. Galatians 2: 20

Again this is a hard lesson for me to learn. That is, I am powerless to carry any of this out on my own. It all starts with faith in the one who gave himself for me. There is nothing I can do or add to it. This same lesson is being learned over and over again in all of the steps I took to get across this raging river we call life. In every step I feared, every step I stumbled, every stumble I took, the Lord lifted me up with His hand.

If the LORD delights in a man's way, he makes his steps firm; though he stumble, he will not fall, for the LORD upholds him with his hand. Psalms 37: 23 - 24

Jesus made this same promise when he taught the disciples about the Holy Spirit.

I will not leave you as orphans; I will come to you.... If anyone loves me, he will obey my teaching. My Father will love him, and we will come to him and make our home with him....But the Counselor, the Holy Spirit, whom the Father will send in my name, will teach you all things and will remind you of everything I have said to you. Peace I leave with you; my peace I give you. I do not give to you as the world gives. Do not let your hearts be troubled and do not be afraid. John 14: 18, 23b, 26 – 27

I think my head is harder than the step stones I am walking on. I do not know how I could have missed this. It all comes down to this: I fear, and have hidden that fear deep inside, even fearing to confront it. And what do we fear? We fear man/society and the way we appear. We try to be everything to everyone leaving no time to be ourselves. We have no peace. Yet here I see that God the Father, God the Son and God the Holy Spirit has made their home within me. The Holy Spirit is acting as counselor, encourager, reminder, all so we can soak in the peace of God's wondrous love.

"Never will I leave you; never will I forsake you." So we say with confidence, "The Lord is my helper; I will not be afraid. What can man do to me?" Hebrews 13: 5b - 6

The writer of Hebrews knew exactly what I was feeling when he quoted the Psalmist. I can understand and allow myself to be who I am in Christ. Not me trying to force myself to be someone else in Christ, for when I do, I become a failure, a hypocrite. Sure, I may not fit exactly what the "churches" say I should be, but I am who I am. For I am the man that God said I am, full of life, compassion and grace that only comes from God. A man willing to be used by God by allowing His love (not mine) to work and live through me. I guess that is why I cry now.

I hear the dying words spoken of Jesus; "It is finished". These are the same words that came to life in me when I accepted the fact that Jesus paid the ultimate price on the cross for my sins. Now though they sound agonizing yet at the same time inviting. It seems as if I can see better, not with my eyes but with my heart. The veil has been completely torn. I suddenly feel the ground shaking and looking down now at this last step stone of love seeing that it is no longer a step-stone but a solid strong foundation. I turn around and see that the step stone path that I just struggled to cross has turned into a solid rock bridge. It is a wide bridge and the step stones have become columns supporting the span. On the bridge there are others both coming and going. Some are preachers, some are teachers, some are givers and some are just the good old plain folk. Each one is looking to the sides and reaching out like they are trying to hold on to someone. So I look again and see that to the sides there are more paths of step-stones with people at various stages on the step-stone path and there are many step stone paths across the river turning into a solid rock bridge just as I am on. This bridge keeps getting bigger and wider as I look.

These people on the bridge are reaching out with prayers, preaching the message of the gospel, with service, teaching, words of encouragement, generosity, leading cheerfully, loving in grace and mercy, and yes sometimes silence. The silence is the quiet encouragement of just being there for them as they stumble along the step stones like I did, I guess as we all did.

We have different gifts, according to the grace given us. If a man's gift is prophesying, let him use it in proportion to his faith. If it is serving, let him serve; if it is teaching, let him teach; if it is encouraging, let him encourage; if it is contributing to the needs of others, let him give generously; if it is leadership, let him govern diligently; if it is showing mercy, let him do it cheerfully. Romans 12: 6 – 8

Going back to chapter 4, I wrote that in Galatians chapter 5 where we are introduced to the fruits of the Spirit, that it seemed hard for me to understand that love was mentioned first. I asked the following questions: Does this mean I have to love first? Do I really have to love, even though I do not feel like loving anyone? Even though I have a hard time loving myself? Well I now have the answer to these; at least I believe I do.

Love that is from God came first and is the anchor column on the one side; *"For God so loved the world"*.

Faith is the anchor on the other side; *"that whoever believes in him shall not perish but have eternal life"*.

In between the two anchors and bridging the columns is Jesus; *"that he gave his one and only Son"*.

I now stand on this bridge of solid rock; Jesus. Jesus is the one that has made all of this possible through his ministry of service to us. After all, it was he who gave his life so that my life might be ransomed from sure death.

Just as the Son of Man did not come to be served, but to serve, and to give his life as a ransom for many. Matthew 20: 28

Other readings for study:

Psalms 18, 23, 1 Corinthians 12

Chapter 14

For This Very reason

In him we were also chosen, having been predestined according to the plan of him who works out everything in conformity with the purpose of his will, in order that we, who were the first to hope in Christ, might be for the praise of his glory. Ephesians 1: 11 – 12

When I started on this path of step-stones it was my effort to take that leap onto the first stone of faith. Or at least I thought it was my effort. It was actually God choosing me; it just took a long time to answer His calling. Then it took me a long time to really understand, that it will all work out for the purpose of God's will so that He might be glorified and I will not.

Let's look at the passage from 2 Peter once again. This is the passage I introduced as the stepping stones in chapter 5.

For this very reason, make every effort to add to your faith goodness; and to goodness, knowledge; and to knowledge, self-control; and to self-control, perseverance; and to perseverance, godliness; and to godliness, brotherly kindness; and to brotherly kindness, love. 2 Peter 1: 5 - 7

I have read some commentaries on this passage and many of them said that these steps do not come one at a time, but instead are worked on all at the same time. I only partially agree with that because I have gone through them one at a time, yet knowing that there was with each, more steps that I would need to take and to work on. I said that at times I felt like I was jumping back and forth between the stones but in reality I was adding to what I had already gone through. I base my thinking that it is a step by step process on the first step in verse five where Peter writes "make every effort to add". This to me indicates that there must be something first before each step or quality.

Then Peter follows up with these words.

For if you possess these qualities in increasing measure, they will keep you from being ineffective and unproductive in your knowledge of our Lord Jesus Christ. But if anyone does not have them, he is nearsighted and blind, and has forgotten that he has been cleansed from his past sins. 2 Peter 1: 8 – 9

Peter writes about possessing these qualities in increasing measure. I think that once you get one step you continue working on that quality while you are achieving the next step. (Maybe the solid rock bridge was under my feet the whole way and I was too hardened to see it.) In my case it went like this:

I first decided to allow God into my life through Jesus. This was my leap of faith. Once I had the faith my own spirit started to be replaced with the Spirit of God, and I felt the conviction when I still treated others as I did before my leap to faith. This was goodness starting to work in me.

Then as I started to see that I was not getting pushback from my old self and actually felt better about myself my faith was increasing as my goodness was being practiced. I started seeking the reasons for my faith in more detail and this was the beginning of my knowledge and in some cases the resurrecting of my knowledge from my childhood learning.

As my faith was increasing along with my acts of goodness my knowledge started to increase as I went to the next step stone of self-control. Yes it takes an active approach to take control of yourself, separating your old self from the new creation that I was in God. This active approach led to perseverance.

As I practiced perseverance, my faith, acts of goodness, knowledge and self control grew greater. With this I could only praise and worship God by living in a godly manner. This took a strong constant effort to shut out my selfishness and to really put others first and not just in words but in my actions.

As I practiced godliness it was my faith that kept me going, and then this turned into brotherly kindness. These two steps were rather difficult for me. It took much conviction of the Holy Spirit for me to understand. I received this conviction as I increased in my knowledge and this in turn led to increases in my self-control and perseverance.

Last step love, not your ordinary love but the love of God, agape. It was faith that carried me through every step even though there were many struggles. It was faith that Jesus was with me, and it was not until the last step that I discovered that I really had nothing to do with it at all. It was the Holy Spirit leading and guiding me and this gave me the peace in my life that I searched for since I was a kid. This peace was Jesus and the Father living in me. See John 14.

And this is his command: to believe in the name of his Son, Jesus Christ, and to love one another as he commanded us. Those who obey his commands live in him, and he in them. And this is how we know that he lives in us: We know it by the Spirit he gave us. 1 John 3: 23 – 24

Since I first started across the stepstones, my spirit has evolved, thank God, from one that was greedy, selfish, worldly,

Step Stones

---

and with no cares, to one that is of God. I still at times want to flesh out and sometimes do, but I am convicted immediately, especially when I treat someone other than being first.

Now I am on the other side from where I started from. I was drawn here because things in life were not working for me very well on the other side. I have found that the path is just as rough and in some cases even more difficult. However I have the peace of Jesus within me, and I know there are many resources for me to draw on. The greatest resource is of course God. This is a direct promise from Jesus himself.

"Come to me, all you who are weary and burdened, and I will give you rest. Take my yoke upon you and learn from me, for I am gentle and humble in heart, and you will find rest for your souls. For my yoke is easy and my burden is light." Matthew 11: 28 - 30

It really is not all that hard. It is just an asking away!

Ask and it will be given to you; seek and you will find; knock and the door will be opened to you. For everyone who asks receives; he who seeks finds; and to him who knocks, the door will be opened. Matthew 7: 7 – 8

When I started going through this process of learning how to love (believe me it is (and still is) a process), I had to ask for a lot of things from God. It is after all the second greatest commandment spoken by Jesus himself. I find myself struggling to make conscious decisions all the time in order to remain in a love frame of mind. With these conscious decisions it always involves a lot of asking.

It's asking God for things like more of you and less of me, show me your will in these matters (whatever is happening at the time).

Many times my asking does not get answered the way I think they should be answered. Sometimes I become disheartened. Then as time goes on, I find myself seeing that God is answering, only in His way, which is always far superior to my way.

Only I can ask; why do my prayers not get answered. It is just like James writes.

Don't they come from your desires that battle within you? You want something but don't get it. When you ask, you do not receive, because you ask with wrong motives. James 4: 1b, 2a & 3a

Or I doubt, because my flesh gets a hold of me.

But when he asks, he must believe and not doubt, because he who doubts is like a wave of the sea, blown and tossed by the wind. That man should not think he will receive anything from the Lord; he is a double-minded man, unstable in all he does. James 1: 6 – 8

Yes, even after all that I have been through, all that I have seen, experienced and the goodness of the Lord that I have tasted, sometimes I still doubt. I then find myself praying and asking for the Lord to help my unbelief, to take this double mindedness away from me. I guess I have always been an unstable person (mind always wandering and going in circles) from my childhood; but I know that with God as my solid rock foundation I am stable. It is just an asking away.

Sometimes my prayers do not get answered because I am not expressing love as God would want me to.

Therefore I tell you, whatever you ask for in prayer, believe that you have received it, and it will be yours. And when you stand praying, if you hold anything against anyone, forgive him, so that your Father in heaven may forgive you your sins. Mark 11: 24 - 25

I find myself in the flesh all too often. It is a struggle that needs to be addressed daily. It makes me wonder if the seventy percent of the Americans who say they are Christian even attempt to address this daily. If they do not, could that be the reason we are in terrible times? Is that why the world sees Christianity as a crutch for weak people? Could it be why so many churches are shrinking and alternative ways (new age, scientology etc.) are gaining? Why so many addictions are growing?

The answer to all of this can be found in the words of Jesus.

I will do whatever you ask in my name, so that the Son may bring glory to the Father. You may ask me for anything in my name, and I will do it. John 14: 13 – 14

If you remain in me and my words remain in you, ask whatever you wish, and it will be given you. This is to my Father's glory. John 15: 7 – 8a

These words were echoed by John so that we can have confidence.

This is the confidence we have in approaching God: that if we ask anything according to his will, he hears us. And if we know that he hears us—whatever we ask—we know that we have what we asked of him. 1 John 5: 14 - 15

I talked about this back in chapter seven when I was going through goodness. But now it strikes home even more so because I feel the struggle within me in a heavier way. I need to make sure that I am acting like one of the sheep on the right and not one of the goats on the left. I realize that all Christians do not have the personalities to go out and seek the lost and teach to fulfill the great commission from Mathew 28. I know I do not and I don't believe God gave me that gift. For me to live the great commission is to behave in a manner that share's the love of God in my actions, words, and thoughts. A touch on someone's shoulder, a firm handshake, a look of understanding and maybe an encouraging word or prayer, letting them know I am there for them in God's strength/grace. In other words I have to be in the will of Jesus, who did everything to bring glory to Father God. If we do so in the same nature, will or name, we too will bring glory to father God.

So let us come boldly to the throne of our gracious God. There we will receive his mercy, and we will find grace to help us when we need it most. Hebrews 4: 16 NLT

Just read the psalms and you will see that David knew this all to well. We are incapable of doing right on our own. Sure we can appear to be right and good but again what are our motives? What is our true heart? We must continue to ask just as David asked over and over again. After all it is just an asking away.

Show me your ways, O LORD, teach me your paths; guide me in your truth and teach me, for you are God my Savior, and my hope is in you all day long. Psalms 25: 4 – 5

I like so many in this world lived my life looking or should I say searching for approval. The approval I wanted was from this world, this society, from family, friends, work, and in how I played, yet I never received it. I finally did get one approval and that was all I need. This approval came from God but only when I accepted the sacrifice of Jesus as one made just for me. When I did that all need for approval was gone. Now I live my life not for approval but in a manner that honors and glorifies the Holy name of our heavenly Father. Not by my efforts or strength but through the Holy Spirits.

So if you are new to Christianity reading this book, or an old timer that struggles with me, or even a long timer that thinks he/she has it all down, I hope this book has awakened something in you. I hope that you will take a close look at your heart, at the truth that can be found only in God, through Jesus. It is the only way for our joy to be complete.

Ask and you will receive, and your joy will be complete. John 16: 24b

Please join me with David in this prayer.

Create in me a clean heart, O God. Renew a loyal spirit within me. Restore to me the joy of your salvation, and make me willing to obey you. Psalms 51: 10 & 12 (NLT)

Now we can also say this prayer for the body of Christ the Church.

Create in your church a clean heart, O God. Renew us with the strength of your spirit. Restore the joy that is found in your salvation so that we are willing to obey you and show the world that your way through Jesus is the only way and the truth. We pray that we will do this, just as Jesus did with compassion, patience, love, and with a servant's attitude all this to glorify your Holy Name. Amen

Now all glory to God, who is able, through his mighty power at work within us, to accomplish infinitely more than we might ask or think. Glory to him in the church and in Christ Jesus through all generations forever and ever! Amen. Ephesians 3: 20 – 21 (NLT)

Other readings for study:

Psalms 100 & 101, Titus 3: 1 – 11, 2 Timothy 2: 14 – 26, 2 Peter 1: 12 – 18, 2 Peter 3